ABOUT TH

KEZIA NOBLE was born in London. She began a music career in 2003, which led to considerable success and a record deal in the US. Kezia believed that a career in the music industry was her destiny, until an out-of-the-blue occurrence in 2006 introduced her to the 'pickup'/seduction community.

One evening, in a trendy bar in the heart of London, a trainer from one of the largest PUA ('pickup artistry') companies in the world asked her to come along to one of their weekend workshops. Kezia was a sceptic at first, but, after witnessing the astonishing results when men followed systemic technical advice in the art of picking up women, she soon became a female coach. Kezia's knowledge and techniques were born from her observations of men considered to be *naturals* – i.e. consistently successful seducers of women – combined with the knowledge obtained from working with some of the PUA gurus.

Kezia has since built a major personal following even among men not previously aware that a seduction community existed. Her expertise has made her the world's premier female PUA trainer, and she is now coming to the attention of the wider public and the mass media.

THE NOBLE ART OF SEDUCING WOMEN

MY FOOLPROOF GUIDE TO PULLING ANY WOMAN YOU WANT

KEZIA NOBLE

JOHN BLAKE

Published by John Blake Publishing Ltd,
3 Bramber Court, 2 Bramber Road,
London W14 9PB, England

www.johnblakepublishing.co.uk

www.facebook.com/Johnblakepub
twitter.com/johnblakepub

First published as 15 Steps To Becoming A Master Seducer in 2010
by Pennant Books.

This edition published in paperback in 2012.

ISBN: 978-1-84358-762-0

British Library Cataloguing-in-Publication Data:

A catalogue record for this book is available from the British Library.

Design by www.envydesign.co.uk

Printed and bound by CPI Group (UK) Ltd, Croydon, CR0 4YY

3 5 7 9 10 8 6 4 2

Papers used by John Blake Publishing are natural, recyclable products made from
wood grown in sustainable forests. The manufacturing processes conform to the
environmental regulations of the country of origin.

Every attempt has been made to contact the relevant copyright-holders,
but some were unobtainable. We would be grateful if the appropriate
people could contact us.

CONTENTS

INTRODUCTION

AUGUST 2003

Saturday night out with the girls. We hadn't seen each other for a few months. I'd been away on a particularly long summer break, and I was eager to see them all again. We'd been friends since college; over the space of a few years we'd cried on each other's shoulders when relationships had gone sour, we'd argued over everything and anything, but we always made up by admitting that we were wrong. We helped each other in our hours of need and shared laughter, holidays and birthdays. In that time we'd grown from girls to adult women.

Here we all were, still friends and celebrating the fact that – through thick and thin, laughter and tears – we remained close.

It was a typical busy Saturday night in London; we were sipping cocktails at one of the most fashionable clubs of the moment. The London party scene was out in full force: beautiful people; famous people; cool people; strange people; rich people; people who wanted to be rich; people who wanted to be famous. And then there were people just out to enjoy life, exactly like we were doing.

We were attracting plenty of male attention and, as a result of that and some lethal cocktails, our egos were getting bigger and bigger.

Men were sending us bottles of champagne; some were brave enough to come over to speak, some tried to dance with us, but all were sent back to their tables with tails firmly between their legs. We even turned down two fairly well-known celebrities, who were particularly annoyed with us for not falling at their feet like most women immediately did.

The thing was, we didn't care. We were on a high, enjoying being together, laughing at the attention we were receiving, and besides – two out of the five of us had boyfriends.

I, however, did not. But I did have my eye on someone at work, in fact I was a little transfixed by him. Any man who spoke to me was automatically and unfavourably compared to him. I remember feeling the need to make a phone call, maybe to check up on him or to shamelessly remind him how much I liked him.

I went outside where it was quieter; it was a particularly pleasant warm night. Perhaps fortunately for me, his phone was off and all I got was his answer machine. His cute voice came on and made me feel warm inside. I left a message on his voicemail and closed shut the phone. As I was about to turn and go back inside the club, I heard a voice from behind me.

"Why are you speaking so loudly?"

I turned around to see a rather ordinary looking guy leaning back in a relaxed manner, with his foot up on the wall behind him. He was kind of cute, but a little short for my liking; his clothes were a bit too casual for my taste too.

"Excuse me?" I replied, feeling sure he'd made a mistake and thought I was one of his friends.

He took a drag from his cigarette and looked into my eyes defiantly.

"You're speaking very loudly, when there's no noise around you. Just thought it was a bit eccentric, that's all." He smiled.

"Yes, sometimes I speak loudly. So what?" I retaliated, looking him up and down in an authoritative manner. But he was right. There was no noise.

"You and your friends have been speaking really loudly all night, that's probably why you're still shouting. Don't worry about it," he laughed.

"I'm not worried about it!" I fired back, getting annoyed with him. I began to search for a cigarette in my bag. I wanted to go but, for some reason, I stayed, probably because I didn't want to seem like I was running scared from him or his remarks.

He came over and lit my cigarette.

"Thanks," I mumbled. I wanted to tell him not to bother, but realised as usual that I had no lighter.

"You're welcome." He smiled, returning to his original position.

"Who's your friend?" he asked

"Which one?"

"The one that all the guys like," he replied, taking another drag from his cigarette.

My mind began to race. We were *all* getting attention. Who was he talking about? I began to feel jealous, which soured my mood.

"The one in the blue dress," he said, noticing my apparent confusion.

"Christina?" I replied.

"Is that her name?"

I began to feel jealous toward Christina. It wasn't anything major, just a pang of mild envy, but I'd never felt anything like that before about her. I didn't like it at all, she was a dear friend of mine, a great girl, but for some reason I resented the fact that she was apparently getting more attention than the rest of us.

Then I realised that this guy may have been winding me up, so I played along.

"Well, I can introduce you to her if you like," I responded.

"That's okay, I can introduce myself if I really want. I'm

Leo, by the way." He put his hand out to mine. I accepted his handshake.

"I'm Kezia."

He began laughing.

"What?" I said, getting increasingly annoyed with him.

"If I tell you, will you promise to not be offended?"

"Promise. Now, what's so funny?"

"It's beautiful, but when I was a kid I can remember that my friend had a hamster with a very similar name – something like Kezla, or Keza."

Although I tried not to, I couldn't help but laugh. My guard had come down.

He took the last drag of his cigarette and rubbed my arm gently, before leaving me standing on my own.

"I'll catch you inside the club later," he said, before turning back and mouthing the words, "And stop speaking so fucking loudly!"

I stood there with my phone still in my hand, wondering what had just happened. How had I been made to experience so many emotions within just a few minutes by a complete stranger who was not my type and was also, frankly, a little too cheeky?

My thoughts were interrupted by the ringing of my phone. It was the guy I had been trying to call before this whole episode. I didn't answer, figuring he could wait for a bit. Isn't it funny how what we consider important can change in just a couple of minutes?

Back in the club, I began discreetly watching my friend Christina and the men all around us. *Are they really looking just at her?* I asked myself.

I began looking for Leo too. I was curious to know where he was, who he was with, but he was nowhere to be seen.

I did, however, notice that one of my friends was in conversation with two very attractive men. She gave me one of our subtle little signs which meant, 'join in.' (We also had a sign for 'help', as well as 'maybe help me soon' – but this was a definite 'come and join us right now!')

I went over. They looked even better close up, and I noticed that one of them smelled so good.

"What aftershave is that?" I asked flirtatiously.

"Issey Miyake," he replied. "I bought it last week."

Then the conversation rapidly took a turn down Tedium Avenue. He began asking me boring questions with little or no interest in my answers. *Yet another man with absolutely no sex appeal and very little charm*, I thought to myself.

It was then that I spotted Leo, standing a few metres away with three attractive women who were laughing with him. I noticed how one kept stroking his arm, deciding she must have been his girlfriend. But then I noticed him taking her hand off, giving her a playful tap on the hand as if to say *enough is enough*. The good-looking but utterly charmless man I was standing next to carried on talking to me about something or other, probably still on about the aftershave he was wearing.

I managed to catch Leo's eye for a few seconds, then looked down to the floor. I looked up again to see him still looking at me. He smiled, and then walked towards the exit with a lighter and cigarette in his hand. I followed.

After I made my excuses to Prince Charmless, I took a moment to think about what I was doing. Why was I following Leo? I had no need to go outside. It was obvious that there was something about him that was drawing me towards him, but what? Eventually I came up with my pretext to explain why I was following him: I would say the guy I was talking to was boring me and I needed to get away from him. It was true, but I also knew that I could have just gone back to my group of friends, or given one of them the 'help' signal and they would have rescued me.

As I came out, I noticed Leo had adopted a similar stance to when he had first spoken to me. But he looked more attractive this time round.

"Hello you," he said,

"Hello to you too," I smiled.

"Give me a cigarette," I demanded, holding out my hand expectantly.

"This is my last one, I'm afraid either you share with me or you ask someone else," he responded, ignoring my hand.

"Okay, I'll share," I smiled sweetly.

"Do you have any illnesses I need to be aware of? If you do, then you have to have the last half." He seemed half-serious.

"How dare you! Of course I don't have any illnesses!"

"Don't get hissy, I have to check. You never know." He smiled, handing me his cigarette.

We began chatting. He told me he was from Essex and was staying in London with his mates for the weekend. He said that the Essex scene was boring, that he was tired of the women there, all orange fake tans looking for a rich guy, but that it seemed to him the girls in central London were the same, minus the orange tan.

"What kind of woman do you like?" I asked, becoming more and more curious.

"Someone who is independent, ambitious, has her life sorted out and is naturally sexy." He said it in such a matter-of-fact way.

"You don't ask for much, do you?" I replied ironically, noticing that the cigarette was nearing its end.

He paused for a moment, absorbing what I'd just said. "I don't understand people who don't have high standards, whether it's with women, men or their everyday circumstances," he said thoughtfully.

"Yes, me too," I agreed eagerly. I didn't want him to think I was one of those people who were just content with their lot in life.

"That's good," he remarked, taking the finished cigarette out of my hand and throwing it across the road. "Come and join me when you're ready."

"Maybe, I'm a bit busy," I replied, well aware that I might have let my guard down too much and needed to appear hard to get.

"As you wish," he said casually, turning his back on me and going back into the club.

It was pointless denying to myself that I was slightly attracted to him. This guy, who was not my type physically, had suddenly somehow become attractive. Not only did he intrigue me but he'd also got me explaining myself, qualifying myself, taking the huge ego he'd first encountered down a peg or two. I felt good when I was around him, it was a strange sensation but highly addictive.

Once back inside the club, I decided that I couldn't be bothered to play any more games. I went over immediately to his table. Straight away he introduced me to the girls at the table, one by one. I noted that he had given them all nicknames, which they all seemed to love. He introduced me as 'Miss Kezia', which I loved too.

He seemed to command the table he was at. I tried discreetly to size up the situation, figuring it could be because he was paying and so everyone was being nice for the free drinks. But I soon realised he wasn't paying at all; in fact it wasn't even his table, it was someone's he had met that evening.

As the night wore on, my friends joined the table; I became slightly worried when Christine joined. Would the blue dress jolt his memory as to why he supposedly spoke to me in the first place? When it didn't seem to, I breathed a sigh of relief.

I ended up sitting closer and closer to Leo; we began talking about what we did for a living, our likes and dislikes and what we both wanted from life in general.

He wasn't like the other guys I usually met. I know it sounds like a cliché, but it was true. He challenged me, he asked me questions I hadn't been asked before, he constantly surprised me with his remarks and he made me think before I spoke. Most men would just agree with me and alter their opinions to fit mine, but he would do no such thing. He provoked me but it felt good. He got me passing his drink to him and lighting his cigarettes for him too. (Cigarettes that one of the girls there had bought for him, I might add.)

Every time I tried to touch him, he would respond as if it was some sort of reward for me that he had to ration. I didn't know how he was getting me to accept all this – but he definitely was.

The most interesting thing is that, at one point in the evening, I began to feel unsure of whether he liked me or not and his challenges started to become a little tiresome.

It was then that it seemed he had sensed my thoughts. He came close to my face, and whispered in my ear, "Did I mention that you look unbelievably sexy every time you stretch out your legs?" I looked back at him, slightly shocked. His reaction was nonchalant, completely unapologetic; he gave an ever so slightly knowing smile and, with that, turned to someone next to him and began chatting as if nothing had happened.

However, he left his hand on my bare leg. I did not remove it. In fact, I relished it. Every so often he would turn back to me and smile, sometimes whispering about certain people at the table. I giggled, enjoying the fact that we had this little secret flirtation going on between us. His hand was constantly on my bare leg.

I eventually excused myself to go to the restroom, giving a sign to one of my friends to join me. I wanted to share this with someone!

In the restroom I began checking my makeup frantically. "How do I look?' I asked my friend.

"You look fine, stop panicking," she said reassuringly. "This really isn't like you, Kezia, to get so focused on one guy."

"What do you mean?" I asked as I applied my lipstick.

"It's so obvious – come on, you are totally into that guy, but he's not even that good looking!"

"I know!" I laughed. "But trust me, he is very sexy, it's like he's so in control and he's very witty, he doesn't take my shit like the others do and he's really funny too." The list was long but the night was short, and I decided not to waste any more time in the restroom.

On the way back to Leo's table, I bumped into the good-looking guy I'd been speaking to earlier.

"Hey, I've been looking for you," he whimpered pathetically.

"Oh yeah, sorry, I've been busy," I quickly replied, looking over his muscular tanned bicep.

"Yeah, I saw, with that short guy, he looks like a plumber or something," he sneered.

I shot him a look of disgust. He was obviously bitter that I'd ignored him in favour of someone else.

"Do you want a drink?" he asked, back to his whimpering, needy voice.

"Bye."

Back at the table, I noticed Leo was gathering his stuff together.

"Where are you going?" I asked

"I'm a bit tired, and I have to go somewhere early tomorrow," he answered casually, taking the last gulp of his drink.

My mind began racing. I was not going to ask him for his number, no way. But at the same time I really wanted to see him again, and the good old 'catch you on Facebook' line would not be available for a few more years yet.

"It was nice meeting you." I smiled, hoping he was going to ask for my number.

He smoothed out the creases in his jacket that we'd been sitting on in the club.

"Look at what you've done," he accused, pointing at a particular crease he couldn't get rid of.

I playfully punched him in the arm.

"Can you iron?" he questioned, as I followed him like a puppy dog to the exit.

"Nope," I responded.

"That's a shame, then there's no point in me getting your number. A woman not only has to have a brain, she's got to do cooking or ironing at least." He was obviously winding me up. I gave him another gentle punch.

He suddenly took my hand, leading me away from the exit and his friends into another room. It was empty, like a chill-out room or a lounge bar, and the music was a lot quieter. I felt butterflies in my stomach. Nothing was predictable with Leo.

He turned to face me, looking deep into my eyes as if he wanted to possess every part of me. It was intoxicating. Before I knew it, we were kissing passionately. My desire for him was becoming greater.

Eventually, that wonderful moment was interrupted by one of the girls, moaning about not feeling well.

"You'd better look after your friend," he instructed politely.

I didn't care about rules and playing hard to get anymore. I wanted to see him again, and if he wasn't going to ask for my number then I'd ask for his. Although normally this would have left a slightly bitter taste in my mouth, I was prepared to take the bitter in order to get to the sweet.

I was about to reach for my phone, but it was as if he had read my mind. He sensed that I was going to break my personal rules on how to behave with guys.

He took out his phone and passed it to me. "Put your number in here," he ordered.

I did as I was told, relieved that I didn't have to go through that whole 'when can I see you again?' scenario.

I tapped in my number and handed it back to him, double-checking every digit was in the correct order. He saved it under 'Kez'.

"I'll drop you a text in a week or so. Gives you time to learn some ironing, so you can come over and fix this jacket," he smiled cheekily.

"Whatever," I sighed, trying to recompose myself.

He then proceeded to give me a long kiss on the cheek, which I tried to turn into a longer, more passionate kiss on the lips.

I failed miserably.

"Go and look after your friend, she looks a bit green," he instructed me (again!), ignoring the faux pas I'd committed in a gentlemanly manner.

I nodded my head and mouthed the word 'goodbye'.

And with that he was gone.

I looked over to my friend, who was indeed turning a funny shade of green. I put my arm around her and took her home, while the other girls decided to stay on in the club.

As I sat in the taxi, watching the funny scenes that go on in London on a Saturday night at 3am, I thought about what had happened. Leo had literally swept me off my feet, all in a matter of hours. He'd gone from being an averagely cheeky guy to someone I wanted to have a relationship with.

I had to tell myself to get a grip. I'd never associated myself with the type of girls who get hysterical over a guy, who start planning the names of babies after the first date. I'd always considered myself more level-headed than that, although of course I'd experienced my fair share of passion (and outright lust). But there was something about this guy that I needed more of.

I began going over the night in my head. Everything I'd said. How I'd said it. Had I come on too strong? Was he going to call me? Would he not call me because I'd tried to kiss him again? Did he think that I was desperate or – worse – easy? Why did he talk to me about Christine? Who were those girls he was with?

As I dropped my friend off, I asked myself the most important question of all:

Did Leo know what he was doing? Was this some sort of technique he was using on me, or was it all natural? I wanted to find out from him.

But I never did . . .

OCTOBER 2006

Three years had passed. I was at the engagement party of Christine (yep, she of the blue dress), who had met her Prince Charming only a year ago and was letting the world know about their happiness. What better way of doing it than throwing a house party?

The five of us girls were together again (plus one, thanks to Prince Charming). There were also quite a few people that I didn't know, but one of them stuck out slightly more than the rest. He was a tall man with long curly hair, a very relaxed expression on his face and a gentle aura about him. His clothes and his general persona could almost be described as New Age. After some brief eye contact, he came over to me and introduced himself as Anthony.

We began chatting; he remarked that my necklace looked kind of ancient Greek and wondered if I was interested in that era of history. It was a funny little question, but refreshing compared to the usual boring chit-chat that goes on at house parties.

We got talking about what we did; he said he was an actor, but was working for a new company that specialised in helping people. Of course I was intrigued.

"How? What type of people?" I asked.

"Men," he replied, eyes fixed to mine, watching for my

reaction. I kept up my poker face. "We help men attract women. We teach them how to talk to women, how to build up sexual tension with them, how to use their assets to the best of their advantage."

I tried not to, but I couldn't help laughing. "No way! You mean like in the film *Hitch*?"

He rolled his eyes. Obviously this was a comparison he had heard before.

"A bit, but that film was more about setting up the circumstances and manipulating events so that one particular guy can get one particular woman. We teach guys to be more confident with women in general." His voice was very matter-of-fact, but he still had this gentle aura which made him seem warm and genuine.

"So you teach *tricks*? Like hypnosis?" I questioned him.

"We teach 'canned openers' – the kind of opener lines a guy can use to make an impact. We also teach NLP, which is not hypnosis but it does use the power of suggestion."

"That sounds dodgy. What on earth is NLP?" I cut to the quick.

"Neurolinguistic programming. You say it's 'dodgy', but take a look at the magazines that you girls read, full of constant tips on how to get men, multiple different ways to get him to fall in love with you too and how to make him want to marry you. If that's not manipulative and dodgy, then I don't know what is."

He'd made a good point. There were loads of magazines and seminars out there to teach a woman how to bag a man, or even how to make him want to father her children. In fact, us females are inundated with tips on the best skills to attract the opposite sex. Open up any one of those monthly woman's magazines and you'll find at least five articles about getting 'him' to propose, or giving 'him' the best blowjob ever to keep 'him' faithful forever.

I wasn't so bothered really about whether manipulation was

involved. I was fully aware that women can be totally manipulative, so if men wanted to turn the tables a little then good for them. I was more concerned with the fact that some combination formula of skills, techniques and NLP couldn't possibly work. Surely attraction was either there or it wasn't?

"You can't seriously tell me that you can grant a 20-stone man with bad breath and a bald patch the power to attract any woman?"

He thought for a moment before answering. "A student like that would make it harder, yes, because he doesn't have what we call a 'natural advantage'. But if you look at some people who have made it in business or entertainment, they might not have had a natural advantage either. For instance, some singers are not very good technically; they might have a just-about-average voice, yet they still make it all the way to number one in the charts. Then there are the thousands of singers out there with amazing voices, and yet they always remain backup vocalists. Natural advantage makes it easier, but it's not a guarantee of success."

I knew what he said was true. I thought back to all the good-looking men I'd met who had a so-called 'natural advantage' and yet had never had many women.

"Our techniques are not a guarantee that anyone can get anybody they choose – that's impossible – but we can help them increase their chances at least."

It was fascinating, I was becoming totally transfixed by the conversation, as other people at the party gathered around him trying to join in. The topic of 'pickup artists' was attracting a large amount of attention. The men in the room were eager to learn some techniques for free, whilst the women were also intrigued, and yet slightly apprehensive at the same time about the whole notion of men *learning* how to attract women.

As far as I was aware, Anthony was the first bona fide 'pickup artist' I'd ever met. But, as fascinating as our encounter was, I needed to get up early next morning and so I began to make a move. I left him entertaining the small crowd which had formed around him.

As I was about to leave, Anthony caught my arm. "Listen," he said. "Think about coming down this weekend. We're having something called a 'boot camp', which is basically a workshop where about 20 or so guys get taught the techniques I was speaking about." He smiled gently.

"I don't think so. Thanks anyway," I replied, making my way to the door. My weekends were precious, I couldn't waste them on workshops for men who were hoping to get lucky.

"I haven't finished," he persisted. "We need girls to act as guinea pigs, we call it the 'hb section', which means 'hot babes'. Our students get to try out their techniques on you, and you give some feedback. We'll pay you too . . ."

THE WEEKEND BOOT CAMP

We were all gathered in a central London bar, me and seven other girls, the bar having been closed off to the public for the boot camp event.

There was a mixture of men there of all different ages and backgrounds. They were all in separate little groups, being trained by five other guys, one of whom I noticed was Anthony himself. He waved to me as I came in the room but was obviously preoccupied with the group he was talking to, so I went over and joined the other women who was sat on the barstools, and who seemed just as intrigued as I was.

I noticed the other trainers were actually fairly average looking guys, but they all had a certain air of confidence about them, they stood differently from the students and had an energy or aura that I'd already come to associate with Anthony. I noticed they all made the absolute most of themselves, with good haircuts, stylish clothes and GOOD SHOES (very, *very* important). I'd anticipated that the instructors would be either ridiculously good-looking model types or creepy geeks, with strange techniques learned from a community of equally strange geeks. It was a really pleasant surprise to find out they were all normal men leading apparently normal lives.

I got talking to a few who told me how they got into the scene. Most said they used to be shy and lacking in confidence around women; their lives had been fine in most respects, except in this one area of dealing with the opposite sex. They all had normal jobs and a good social life, but at some point in their life they had been fairly hopeless with women and had decided to do something about it.

"But how did you find out about all this?" I asked an instructor called Phillip, who went under the nickname 'Sicily'.

"In America it's big business," he answered, eyeing up a passing waitress with particularly long legs.

"Ever heard of Neil Strauss? Mystery? *The Game*?"

"Nope," I answered. They sounded like a bunch of Bond villains to me.

"Well, Neil Strauss is like the godfather of the 'pickup community', he wrote a book called *The Game* which is the bible of pickup artists. Once I read that book my eyes were opened, and it spawned a whole community on a much larger scale than over here. In the US there are major pickup artists that do seminars, coaching and have their own TV shows – they are literally celebrities out there. Anyway, once I heard about this small community in England I became a part of it. The rest is history."

I took in all he said. Although he was trying to be casual, his enthusiasm was very obvious. "But you, for instance, you seem really confident. I can't see you having a problem picking up women," I said.

"You should have seen me before – I was terrible, like really bad. I didn't even kiss a girl until I was 19, now I've slept with 40 women." He was most definitely boasting now.

"How old are you?" I asked.

"21." He took great pride in telling me this. If it were true, if this guy had gone from a being a pumpkin to a prince, from zero to 40 women, in the space of two years, then maybe these techniques were more helpful than I'd originally thought.

"You got all your confidence from this book, *The Game*?" I pursued, noting from the corner of my eye that the students were now heading over toward us.

"It's like learning a new language, you can't just learn it all from a book. So I joined the community, which is fairly small here in London but growing really rapidly," he waved his hands around the room, to demonstrate his point.

"There are a few fairly good instructors in the UK who have taught me some stuff. We started going out together, working on our game [I realised then that when these men said 'game' it meant their talents in attracting woman], trying out skills, creating new ones. I improved my fashion sense, got contacts, got my teeth fixed, worked on my body language and conversation skills, and then slowly, slowly, the women started coming in. When that happens your confidence naturally grows too."

He seemed very honest about who he was and who he used to be, which was cool. But it was hard to imagine that this guy was ever that bad; he was certainly more confident than the men I usually spoke to.

"Looks like it's back to work," he smiled, spotting the students waiting nervously in the wings to speak to the girls. Phillip/Sicily – who took his name from the birthplace of his granddad, who was apparently a bit of a Casanova – gathered the girls around in a huddle. He placed himself in the middle of us, like a football coach when he gives out instructions to his team.

The other girls were very pretty, two of them were what one could only describe as intimidatingly beautiful, the others well above the average type of girl you see in the street. *These poor guys probably can't even talk to some plain Jane in the office, let alone these girls,* I thought.

"Right, ladies, here's the deal," began Phillip, relishing every moment. Here he was, the self-confessed ex-geek, telling a group of hot girls what to do. I noticed his t-shirt kept rolling up, showing off an ethnic-style tattoo (maybe North African or Indian) on his gym-pumped left bicep. I could tell he was just aching to be asked what it meant. Was this another well thought-out technique?

"The students are going to chat you up as if you're a girl they met at random in the bar. I want you ladies to ignore the instructors who are hanging around them, like me, and to make the scenario as natural as possible. At the end we would like your feedback."

The girls nodded their heads in perfect synchronisation. His eyes lingered on the tall blonde from Sweden. (A cliché perhaps, but true.)

"I like your tattoo," she said, pointing to his bicep. "What does it mean?"

This stuff was *good*. But some of the students were absolutely hopeless, they were so desperately trying to remember some awesome line they'd heard that they forgot how the whole point was to seem relaxed and confident. To be fair, there were some who were not so bad, just like the typical guy you meet anywhere – fairly quiet until he has a drink.

"I've never done this without at least a few pints," one of them whispered to me.

One of the other guys used the opener, "Does my shirt look gay?'" To which I replied honestly, "Yes, it does, you should change it."

The poor guy looked shocked. "Umm, uh," was his response. He turned to the instructor, who whispered something to him.

He turned back to me and smiled.

"That's what I thought, but don't you think gay guys have much better style than straight guys?"

"Yes," I answered. (It's true, gay guys on the whole do look a lot better than straight men.) This was better than the student's first stammering response, and as a result we got into a longer conversation. The trainer was pleased and gave him the thumbs up.

The students were also trying out a technique called 'kino', which I understood to be a type of skill men can develop whereby they create comfort with a girl, by touching her subtly, so as to break down her shield and get her used to a more physical interaction. Unfortunately, there was one man who was overusing the kino technique, and as a result of his enthusiasm he spilled some of my drink on me. As I tried to clean off the spillage, he just stood there and looked at me, totally stuck on the spot and unable to move. It seemed he just hadn't been fed the right lines to respond to it.

After two hours of the good, the bad and the ugly, everyone was asked to sit down. It was feedback time. I noticed that a couple of the girls kept giggling, obviously sharing a joke about one (or maybe all) of the students. One of the instructors quietly asked them to hide their amusement. "These guys don't mind honest feedback, but not humiliation," he politely said. They stopped straight away.

Finally, when everyone was sitting down in a semicircle, a tallish man with fairly long dark hair walked in and stood in front of the audience. He was noticeably a lot more relaxed and had more of an air of natural confidence than the other instructors. No tattoos, no blonde highlights, no jewellery, just slightly dishevelled plain clothes, as if he'd just got out of bed. The only expensive thing he was wearing was his leather jacket – a beautiful brown classic that gripped his body perfectly.

"Hey guys," he began, his voice soft but by no means shy. "I'm Gambler." I noticed that a few of the students started whispering.

"I run PUA Training, and, like many of you, only two years ago I was totally hopeless with girls." He began a long story about how hard it had been to change; he spoke about how the techniques and skills he had perfected could be applied to not only seduction and attraction, but to the student's life in general. He went on to say that attracting good-looking women went hand in hand with self-respect and displaying high value.

This I felt was a much more interesting take. Although I could see the necessity of good openers and anecdotes for beginners, and that a quirky necklace or tattoo might make a good little prop to encourage the girl to make a comment or provoke her to ask questions, it wasn't enough to help these guys take it to the next level.

I've always believed that you never finish learning, never stop improving yourself, and there is always the option of taking whatever you do in life a step further. This was apparently something that Gambler believed in too, as he introduced this school of thought under the heading of 'natural game' – that is, coming across as a natural seducer, and not noticeably as a pickup artist.

I immediately knew that this would be the real heart of the course. Natural game can help with building confidence, managing people in different situations, dealing with people in business or friendships, not only with seduction. (I KNOW this for a fact, because my own students have since told me about it.)

The students sat completely transfixed, taking down notes at the speed of light.

When Gambler finished he gave the signal for the girls to give their feedback; the men were waiting with baited breath for our little pearls of wisdom. Unfortunately, after Gambler's great speech what the girls had to offer was pretty weak.

The first girl pussyfooted around, more concerned about being likeable and collecting her money than being honest. "I think you were all really great," she said, lying through her teeth. A few of the students rolled their eyes.

"Well done," said another girl, equally mealy-mouthed.

Finally, one girl was a little more outspoken, giving a more honest kind of feedback. "I think some of you need to be more confident, you need to stop looking so nervous; maybe you should relax your hands a little so that you don't start twiddling your thumbs."

I noticed that the guys didn't react badly to her opinion. In fact it was quite the opposite, they were sick of girls being sweet and pitying their apparent lack of confidence, they obviously wanted some no-holds-barred feedback.

Then the attention of the room turned to me, the last girl. *Fuck it,* I thought, *I will never see anyone here again. I'm going to be brutally honest, but I'm going to make sure my criticism is constructive too.*

"Man in yellow shirt," I began, "you asked if me if your t-shirt looked gay. When I said it did, you showed how you didn't anticipate that as an answer. You then had to go to the instructor to find the perfect response – well, he's not always going to be there, so for future reference always expect the unexpected, there will always be at least a few great responses you can go with. Don't be too dependent on the opener, concentrate more on what comes after."

He picked up his notepad and began writing down my words, the others doing likewise. This was the first time they'd written notes since Gambler's speech.

I continued. "To the man who spilt my drink on me . . ." He

looked up, embarrassed. "It's not so much the actual spillage that I was bothered about, it was the fact that you just stood there and did nothing. Don't you think that it was a perfect opportunity for you to take the lead, to show what a gentleman you are? You could have at least handed me a napkin or offered to get me another drink, anything, at least it would have made the conversation flow rather than just cutting it short."

I turned to the rest of the men. "If something like this happens, you have two choices: either you create an uncomfortable moment, or you laugh about it and turn that initial negative situation into a positive outcome. You could take the lead and maybe take her arm gently, leading her to a place where you can assist her in cleaning the mess. It's also a great way to get her away from her annoying friends." The students laughed; I was relieved that they weren't taking the advice badly.

"As for this kino thing, it needs to come off more naturally. I understand why you're doing it, but some of you were resting your hand on my arm for too long and you kept looking at where you were going to put it first, making the situation seem really quite weird. Maybe if you spoke about an item of jewellery and then touched it, it would be a better way to get into her space."

Looking back now, this was very generic advice compared to what I now give to my students, but nonetheless they seemed to welcome the novelty of honest female feedback.

I noticed Gambler in the background, slowly edging closer to me; it was my signal that time was up.

"Anyway, guys, well done for taking the first step, I for one know how difficult and frightening us girls can be." I'm known for being a *particularly* difficult woman. And so are my friends! "Keep practising and get used to that fear, and in time you will desensitise yourself to it."

I was surprised to find a warm round of applause filling the room.

Gambler took over and told everyone to go for a half-hour break. I put on my coat, ready to get paid and go back to my real world, but at that moment one of the students came up to me with a notepad and pen.

"Are you a trainer, Kezia?" he asked shyly.

"A what? . . . oh, an instructor? No, not at all," I laughed.

"That's a shame, I wanted to book a session with you."

It turned out that on the website of PUA Training there was a page where the instructors gave their details and the students could pay for their time. These 'one-on-one' sessions seemed to be really popular. A few other students came up to me with some more questions and also enquired whether they could book me for a one-on-one. Eventually, I managed to get away and collect my money for the two hours.

"See you next week," Gambler said casually as he handed me the money.

"Next week?"

"Yeah. We're having another weekend session and you did really well, so it'd be cool if you came down again."

Eventually I was going to the boot camps every weekend. The girls I'd originally worked with came and went, most of their feedback pretty vague, and it seemed to me they wanted to come across as likeable and not to hurt the students' feelings. (It's true that women are often people-pleasers.)

As time went on I began listening more to feedback from the other instructors, which to me was fascinating. They were using terminology and code words that I'd never heard before, such as 'I.O.I's', which I learned translates as 'Indicator of Interest', meaning signs that a girl gives when she develops an interest in a guy.

An 'HB 7' was jargon for a 'hot babe who is literally seven out of ten', whereas an 'HB 10' was considered to be stunningly hot.

'AMOG' meant 'Alpha Male of the Group', a guy that everyone thinks is cool and is always the social centre of the room. AMOG could also be used as a verb to describe when a man is deliberately intimidating other men around him, by making them feel less popular or less successful than he is.

I began attending the whole weekend at the boot camps, listening to the other instructors give their well-polished talks and demonstrations. I realised that what had seemed like a joke to me at first was actually something that was really helping men attract women. I was convinced from the results that I witnessed that attraction could be taught and chemistry could be made in an almost systematic manner. (I regard 'chemistry' as a fanciful word we use to describe those unexplained emotions, or sparks of sexual energy, that we feel for another person.) It was a real eye-opener.

Eventually I got an email from Gambler, asking me to come and meet him during the week for a chat. We met in a small café in Soho, not far from where the boot camps were held. He had a file with him and a laptop; this was obviously not just a cosy catch-up.

"I haven't had a chance to really talk to you properly, I mean about the company, where we are going and what we want from you," he said in his usual casual manner.

I was puzzled. "Uh . . . do I need to know this kind of information?" I asked, stirring the sugar around in my coffee.

"Well, we want you to be a team player and to work fulltime, so I think you *should* know it, don't you?" Again, he said it as if it was all just off the cuff.

I tried not to show my surprise, but it's pretty hard to hide it from someone who's a master of body language and an expert at reading people.

In my head, this had always been just a little weekend job. Fair enough, it was extremely interesting and made for fantastic conversation at dinner parties, but it was never anything that I could consider fulltime. Not only that but my current job was very well paid, so money was not necessarily an enticement either.

Gambler could sense my apprehension.

"When I say fulltime, it doesn't mean nine-to-five in an office, it means you become part of the team, we put you on the website as a female trainer, you work with residentials [students who stay with Gambler for a week], you can have private one-on-one sessions with students, ex-students or even someone who just goes to the website. You can have students in your own time, after work or at the weekends, as long as it doesn't interfere with the boot camps." His phone began to ring, but after a quick glance at the screen he switched off the phone. (Probably just a girl.)

I explained about the money at my job and how much time this new job would take up. He assured me that very soon I would be doing better than I already was, and that PUA Training was providing one of the world's major pickup training courses (it was already the biggest in Europe by a mile).

"The students love you," he said, then pondered his statement further. "Actually, they hate you, but only because you tell them the truth. And then they love you."

I laughed. I knew I was getting a reputation as one of the harshest girls in the HB section.

"Seriously though, your advice is so spot on, you're not afraid to say it as it is and you look pretty good too."

"What does that have to do with it?" I asked.

"Well, most of these guys are nervous about even talking to Jane from down the road, so when they practise on you in role play etc, and you're wearing those tight-fitting clothes and have this glamorous air about you, it starts to bolster their confidence. I say to them sometimes, 'Look, if you can talk to Kezia and beat your nerves then you'll be able to do it with most other girls.'"

I ruminated on my thoughts for a while. *Should I be doing this? Should I put more effort into it and start looking at it as a proper fulltime job? Can a female trainer succeed in this industry?*

I'd always been aware of the lack of female input to the 'pickup community'. There were a few wing girls on the scene who'd offer the usual vague pieces of advice, such as 'be yourself', 'smile more', 'be more confident', and although their intentions were good the students felt that they were more concerned about coming across as likeable rather than giving them detailed and honest feedback that would really help. My tough love approach was what they wanted.

"I need you to start learning public speaking too," he said, interrupting my thoughts. "We will be doing some pretty big summits soon, are you cool to talk to over 300 people?"

I didn't know the answer, since I had never actually done it before.

"I'll put you in touch with some guys who are professional public speakers, they'll coach you. Oh yeah and there will be some media work too – newspapers, radio, TV."

I realised he had presumed my answer was yes. I agreed. This was going to be great!

*　　*　　*

Eight months later I would leave my job. As Gambler had predicted, at first it wasn't taking up that much time, but as the business grew so did my list of students. We were getting more and more media coverage and the summits were always sold out, as were the boot camps. At first we had a residential staying in the 'PUA mansion' nearly every week, but soon we were having up to four at a time. It was becoming impossible for me to hold down both jobs, and in the end I chose to work for PUA Training fulltime.

When I left PUA Training I had managed to learn a lot working for them. I was able to see what they were doing right and, of course, what I felt they were doing wrong too, which helped me set up my own company with a new team of experts.

I was becoming one of the most in-demand trainers, and the more students I helped the more I learned too. I began formulating new techniques and skills that the other trainers were not using. I was the only woman doing this, and an honest female opinion, followed by detailed advice that really works, was near-impossible to find.

MARCH 2008: *DÉJÀ VU*

I was at one of our PUA super-summits, where we had pickup artists joining us from around the world.

A lot of people in the industry were there; I couldn't believe how big it had actually all become. There were a few American trainers there too who were treated like semi-celebrities (in fact some of them were *actual* celebrities), which seemed to be a taste of things to come for us. Students were busy trying to talk to them and some of the pickup artists were busy trying to talk to me. Since getting a name for myself I was apparently considered to be a bit of a prize amongst the PUAs, since I know every trick in the book and have the reputation of being a tough girl to crack. It's become a kind of game between them to see who can get me first. It's quite amusing.

After the summit we all went to a club in the West End. Along with the more famous pickup artists came their entourages, consisting of active or aspiring instructors. Most were fairly good but some were definitely still in the very early stages of their careers. One of the better ones was called Mickey, who was from California, and boy did he look Californian – blonde hair, blue eyes, a Malibu tan and a body he must have worked hard for in a gym since birth.

He was trying to get my attention but, to be honest, I was not in the mood to start flirting with possible future colleagues, no matter how much champagne I'd been drinking. No matter how good looking he was either.

I remembered suddenly that I needed to make a phone call. The club was too loud, so I stepped out into the chilly night air, shivering pathetically outside where the smokers were all huddled together, complaining about the smoking ban that had been introduced a few months before.

Finally I got through to the person I needed to talk to. They were hassling me about something or other, I can't remember what, but I do remember that it began to annoy me. As my temper grew, my voice began to rise. I noticed a few people turning their attention towards me. I lowered my voice, but only slightly.

"Look, stop your shit, I'm at a club and don't need this right now!" was the last thing I said before I slammed shut the phone.

"Why do you talk so loudly?"

Déjà vu. Leo?

Nope, it was Mickey.

Suddenly, questions filled my mind. Mickey had unintentionally triggered my memories of Leo, and I wanted to pick his brains about a few things,

I met up with Mickey the next day for lunch, before he went back to LA. I began to tell him the whole story about Leo. How it was uncanny – now that I thought about it – that their opening lines were exactly the same; not only that, but Mickey was doing several other things that were exactly what Leo had been doing that night: such as getting the women around him to pour his drink, or to massage his shoulders as he talked to another girl.

Having been a trainer in the pickup community for quite some time by now, I'd seen this display a thousand times before by other artists. In fact, I was teaching these exact skills to my students, but it took that opening line to jolt my memory.

It was obvious to me now that, when Mickey told me I was talking too loudly on the phone, he did it in order to break down my ego. After that he'd even told me he used to have a snake with a name like mine – which of course was complete fantasy, and also uncannily similar to what Leo had told me about his friend's hamster.

I'd noticed during the course of the evening that the similarities between Mickey and Leo did not end there. Mickey also kept moving the girl's hand off him when she got too pally in the club. It's a classic technique that pickup artists use a lot, to make the girls feel as if they have to 'earn' the right to keep touching the guys. It also helps ensure that the interaction doesn't fall into the 'friends' zone' – i.e. in a friendship with a girl but without any way to escalate it – too soon.

I questioned Mickey as we finished off our lunch. "I understand the part where you said mine was the name of a pet you once had, it was obviously a way to break down my ego."

"Well, you have a big ego to burst. Come on, I could have said a pet rat or dog – at least a snake is cool." He smiled.

"True, I guess it's better than a hamster."

"Huh?"

"Forget it," I laughed. He looked at me as if I was slightly mad.

"But the more I think about it, the more sure I am that Leo was a pickup artist," I said, noticing Mickey was getting slightly annoyed that the conversation was still around this guy.

"In my opinion, it sounds like he could have been using techniques," Mickey said, leaning in and talking with a quiet voice that made it seem as if we were discussing top secret information. "But the only reason I doubt he was a pickup artist is because 'pickup' was not widely known back then."

It was a very good point.

Mickey looked at his watch. He had a plane to catch and probably thought my invitation for lunch was going to lead to something more than an interrogation about his techniques. I'm sure he was hoping to be the first in the community to sleep with me – but, being a true professional, I keep my love life completely separate from my work.

But Mickey had been helpful in trying to determine whether Leo had indeed been a pickup artist, or if he was simply a natural. I thought about it on my walk home. By the time I'd reached my front door I'd come to the conclusion that he must have been a natural. After all, it's guys like Leo who have been the inspiration for pickup artists around the world.

The original pickup artists – guys who previously couldn't get women, or wanted to improve on what they already had – studied, replicated and mastered what the naturals did. They made what they learned from them into systems and techniques, so that other men in the same position as they were can learn how to be successful with women too.

These systems have expanded greatly from the days when they first began. Techniques are always being created and developed, to the point at which no one can tell the difference between the naturals and the artists. At some point in their lives the artists took a look at the guy who gets all the women; rather than hating him they chose to admire him and, rather than sticking to being bad with women out of habit, they recognised that if one human being can do something, then another can consciously imitate it.

Having taken control of this particular part of their lives, some have applied the same attitude to other areas of their life too. A good example of this is Gambler. From developing his skills with women he also developed his social skills too; he has changed his outlook on life and become more confident on the outside. As for whether his confidence ran deep, is a different thing entirely. Although, since writing this book, I hope he has developed his inner confidence more than when I knew him, when I used to work for his company.

A lot of my students have often written to thank me for helping them, not just with women but also with the other areas of their lives completely unrelated to pickup – such as their social group, or their work or business lives. They understood that taking control was the single most important factor they could learn from all of this, and I certainly agree.

As a master trainer I'm now in the position where I can break down everything Leo did that night in 2003: the way he controlled the frame of the conversation; the way he used the punishment and reward system; the push-pull technique; the way he made me feel; the clever way in which every time I touched him was made to feel like some sort of honour; the fact that he could sense how I was feeling, and was able to seize the moment and act upon it.

Leo, in my opinion, was one of those men who can make chemistry naturally; Gambler, Mickey, Sicily and all the rest of the good pickup artists I know are also creating chemistry between men and women, but will admit that they are using learned techniques. Yet they are now just as successful as the 'naturals'.

In this book, I'm going to share with you the secrets of a natural and the secrets of a pickup artist. I've decided to explain it in 15 steps. So why 15? Why not ten, or 100?

Initially I wanted to make it ten, but found it was impossible. There was too much to include after training 2000 students. I've had students come to me with all manner of problems and sticking points. There were the students with virtually no social awareness or social skills at all, with no idea how to talk to their best friend, let alone to a woman. There have also been students who had experienced some degree of psychological abuse when they were kids, or from ex-partners who unfortunately made their lives a living hell, and as a result left their confidence in pieces.

These were very difficult cases, and in helping them I learned a great deal myself. I feel honoured that some of my students trust me enough to tell me stories that they've never shared with anyone else, or have been brave enough to cry.

The extreme cases have pushed me to find ways to help these men find at least a partial solution to their problems. This is also why I found it impossible to get all the information gathered over three years across to you, the reader, in anything less than 15 steps.

On the other hand, the reason I haven't exceeded 15 steps is that you'll find 'sub-steps', as well as plenty of anecdotal examples and real-life stories, which will explain and demonstrate each step clearly.

Using this book, I'm hoping you will learn to master the art of 'creating chemistry' and, as a result, increase your success rate with women. Whether you want to simply have the choice of better quality women (in terms of looks, personality or status), to make multiple conquests or to find one special woman to share the rest of your life with, creating a personal chemistry is the first and most important step you can make toward your particular goal.

Each step has been placed in its sequential order, and my advice to you is that, before reading through the steps, make a small promise to yourself that you'll avoid the temptation to skip any just to get to a certain technique you've wanted to learn for ages. This is is because there will be references to the other steps that came before, and it will make no sense to you if those sections have not been read. So please, no skipping – read this book from start to finish!

And one final note before we get underway: if I ever bump

Kezia talking at an 'attraction seminar'.

Kezia being filmed for one of several TV documentaries on PUA Training.

Kezia at one of the 2009 'attraction summits'.

into Leo I will definitely ask him whether he was, in fact, a natural or a pickup artist. Regardless of his answer, I'll be sure to let him know there's always a place at PUA Training if he ever needs a job . . .

· STEP ONE ·
UNDERSTANDING CHEMISTRY

Master seducers are not the men who hope for chemistry.

ROMANTICISM VERSES PRACTICALITY

WHEN IT COMES to the subject of seduction, I initially really struggled with this. Does personal chemistry really exist? Can it be taught? Are you born with it? Or is it just a fanciful word we use to describe certain feelings we get when we meet someone we're attracted to? If so, does chemistry only occur by chance? Is it a force so great that we are unable to control it? Or is chemistry the compound result of certain factors that we have varying degrees of power over – such as the timing, knowledge, logistics and attitudes that may create an almost perfect series of events?

Understating the role of an immeasurable force like personal chemistry is like ignoring the power of oxygen: oxygen is invisible to the naked eye, yet its power is so great that we need it in order to stay alive. So to disregard the chemistry of attraction, feelings and emotions is like saying that oxygen is not a scientifically measurable chemical which can be broken down and explained in intricate detail, but simply a form of magic!

This is the type of ignorance that can hold back your game. In time I began to understand the causes and factors which create the requisite chemistry, how they work, why they work and, most of all, how they can be controlled, manipulated and used for your benefit. Possessing this knowledge will ultimately free you from such ignorance forever; it will separate you from the defeatists who believe personal attraction is simply a form of magic and that there is no real control over it – and no way of creating it.

Throughout history, many women and men have argued that there is no way to create an attraction, that the personal chemistry for it either exists or else it does not. I beg to differ. I consider these people to be hopeless romantics who either get lucky or spend their lives waiting for that unexplained magic to just happen one day. If and when it doesn't happen like the fairytales promised them, they become bitter and consequently blame everyone and everything – except themselves.

I totally believe that you can posses the same power as those men out there who can have practically any woman they want, but you need to accept the first rule of pickup: taking control.

This first step will guide you through taking control in relation to your state of mind, your body language, your self-image and your conversation skills. Without understanding the power of control, you will not be able to fulfil the other two elements of pickup which will be introduced to you later.

The successful seducer has learned that the outcomes of his interactions are very much in his control, and without control he will rely on only the fickle game of chance.

The following are two example of how the sensation of chemistry can be built up; the first demonstrates the slow build-up and the second demonstrates the rapid build-up. Each of these examples are taken from my personal experiences, and hopefully by sharing them with you I can explain the importance of taking control and adopting a practical viewpoint rather than a romantic (i.e. less realistic) one.

SLOW BUILD-UP OF THE 'CHEMISTRY SENSATION'

I was working in an office a few years back, it was a typically grey environment with 15 other people. Nothing exciting ever happened; lunch would be either at our desk or in the café down the road, and the drinks after work on a Friday were invariably at the Red Lion pub opposite. Amongst my fellow colleagues there was a man who worked a few desks from mine named Carl. He was average looking, not really my type, and from what I knew of him it appeared his interests differed from mine too. He was also from an older age group.

For one year I was as indifferent to him as he was to me. If I was off work for a few days he'd be the last to realise, and often I'd forget to even say 'hello' to him in the morning.

One day, whilst standing by the office photocopier, me and Carl were having our usual uninteresting chit-chat. But this time he said something that made me laugh; it was a little odd, very dry and hit my personal funny bone right on target. (Gambler always says I have a Clockwork Orange *sense of humour, whatever that means!) I laughed with him for a few minutes until we realised our giggles were disturbing others in the office. Although at the time I thought nothing of it, there was something very small happening on another level. I had begun to look at him slightly differently; it was an extremely delicate shift in my perception of him, but nonetheless that tiny shift would cause ripple effects.*

We began to share more conversations together, mainly

humorous ones. I noticed that people began rolling their eyes when we laughed together, as our interactions had become very private and exclusive. The conversations eventually became more serious and we began to get to know each other better, finding more in common than we could ever have anticipated. But if you had asked me there and then if I fancied him, I would still probably have said 'no'. Although my subconscious was very aware of what was developing, my conscious mind was still oblivious.

As time went on I found myself looking forward to lunch breaks more than before, solely so that we could spend that precious hour talking to each other. Even those previously tedious drinks at the Red Lion were looked forward to with anticipation.

A few weeks later Carl had to go away for a week, just as he'd often done in the past, except this time I remember feeling sad rather than indifferent. Whilst he was away I would stare absentmindedly at his empty desk; going for drinks and lunch breaks seemed less important. Even the upkeep of my appearance was temporarily put on hold, at least for work. I remember clearly the day when he came back – I gave him a huge hug and felt incredibly warm inside.

A few weeks later I got into an argument with one of the newer office workers. This man was a nasty piece of work, and the argument became very heated; he became intimidating and I felt myself backing down. Carl had witnessed the argument and, before the man had even finished his tirade of abuse, he intervened. He stood between me and the bully, his back facing me, and told the man in no uncertain terms that, if he didn't back down and stop the abuse, then Carl's fist would be going through his head and hitting the wall behind him. The man was momentarily about to turn his anger straight onto Carl, but when he saw how serious he was he backed down almost instantly.

Carl turned to me and asked if I was okay. I remember his voice was strong yet sincere; as I nodded in the affirmative, he gently touched the side of my cheek with the back of his hand. Only at that moment did I admit to myself that I was extremely attracted to this man, and wanted to be with him.

So, let's break down this series of events and see what happened in order to create that 'chemistry sensation'.

The moment Carl told me that joke, he created a seismic shift in my perception of him. I was instantly propelled into a positive frame of mind. However brief the moment, it was still powerful enough for me to associate him with that positive sensation every time I saw or thought of him from thereon. When we start to associate positive feelings and events with another human being, we are prepared to overlook their faults and become more eager to recognise their positive attributes.

Now, maybe if Carl had not stood up for me against the bully that day and had instead chosen to be a coward, turning a blind eye, then that subsequent small event could have ultimately jeopardised that earlier all-important moment in my mind which had positioned me between friendship and love. However, he chose to take control and seize the moment. But if Carl had never told me a joke which made me laugh for ten minutes, I'd never have seen him as anything else but 'the man that sits three desks away from me'.

The main point I'm making here is that the attraction I felt for Carl was not built on chemistry. In actual fact, it came out of a series of events which created two ideally synchronised frames of mind; as a result of that, the attraction was created, and the chemistry was a by-product of the attraction.

This story can be regarded in either one of two ways: firstly, it can be written off as just another 'office romance', which came about after two people had become attracted to each other through a deep-rooted chemistry; alternatively, it can be unromantically broken down into extremely fine detail and explained rationally.

Always adopt the second perspective.

To say that any of your past relationships or sexual conquests were built on chemistry can ultimately make the memory more romantic, but it also makes it unexplainable and therefore impossible to learn from – or to replicate.

You might be thinking, "Well, that's all very well, but what about other situations where people see each other across a darkened dance floor? The raw heat of animal attraction rips through them and, within an hour, they are in bed, ripping each other's clothes off. That can only be chemistry, right?"

Wrong!

It is exactly the same as before, but on a shorter timescale. I see it as rapid build-up of the 'chemistry sensation'. It still possesses all the ingredients of the above story, such as the synchronised frames of mind and a near-perfect series of events: in this case, at least one person taking some form of control. The dance-floor scenario is only different in that it contains the 'natural advantage' factor, which is when someone possesses the physicality that appeals to the woman he wants.

We will be addressing the latter point further on in the book. Until then, here is another story of the chemistry sensation, but this time it happened within a much more rapid timeframe.

RAPID BUILD-UP OF THE 'CHEMISTRY SENSATION'

I remember going out one Thursday night when I was 21. I was feeling great, I'd just had a great week away on vacation and I was with a friend who I hadn't seen for ages. My spirits were high and

I happened to look fabulous that night – thanks to a new haircut and a glowing tan.

We went to a club I'd never been to before, as my friend said it was great. It was fairly new and based in central London. From the outside it looked like a huge glass elevator, with fluorescent neon lights creating strange shapes around the main entrance, making it seem like a set out of Star Trek.

After we walked in and absorbed the general ambience of the place, it could not have been more than ten minutes before I noticed a man at the bar who was very much my physical 'type'. Judging by the way he looked at me, I was his type too. After a little flirtatious eye contact, and the old routine of looking away and back again, he eventually introduced himself. I remember clearly that his aftershave wasn't very nice, it was musky and woody whereas, like many young women, I prefer a fresher scent. But he seemed confident and, like me, he was in a positive frame of mind.

We had a few drinks together and some light conversation. It turned out he was very much an Alpha male – he knew what he wanted and he knew how to get it. He asked me what my favourite song was; I told him and he laughed, saying it was an unusual choice for a girl ('Theme from Ghostbusters' *– hey, it was said as a joke!), but since the DJ was his friend he arranged to have it played. As we danced to my favourite song I felt incredibly turned on by him, and by the moment. We kissed, and the rest of the night will remain my own private business.*

Many people would say this is a classic case of chemistry. But, in actual fact, what we have here is literally two people whose eyes met across a busy room and, before they knew it, they were overtaken by uncontrollable passion, almost as if their bodies had taken control of their minds. Of course, this is once again an over-romanticised version of events. As you know by now, the realistic version is far more helpful – and usually far more accurate!

So, let's break this down again. First of all, at the start of that night I was already in a positive frame of mind before even encountering this man. Most likely, if I'd been in a bad mood or was feeling stressed, it would have undoubtedly come across in my face and body language, instantly making me less attractive – with or without that tan and haircut! It's important to recognise that 'state' is nearly always a more important factor than physical appearance.

Now, the second part of the story is where 'natural advantage' plays its role. If, like Carl, the man had not happened to be my type, then yes, he would have gone relatively unnoticed. But in this case he was my type and this advantage was compounded by my state of mind. And if *he* had been in a negative state of mind, it would have been game-over from very early on. (Remember Leo, who was not physically my type and therefore didn't have the natural advantage factor – but he still created chemistry within a rapid timescale!)

I've seen some absolutely breathtakingly gorgeous men, but if their attitude stinks, or they are on a low, or have a negative state of mind, then they automatically become like a Venus flytrap – nice to look at, but I wouldn't touch it with a bargepole!

So, whereas Carl had needed to create that shift in my mind with his sense of humour, the man in the club had done the same job on a much more rapid timescale, thanks to his natural advantage (his physicality) and the positive state of mind he oozed that evening. As you'll recall, I mentioned not liking his aftershave – I can also remember that he didn't have very nice hands either, and as for his shoes, I really hated them! But in spite of all of this, I overlooked his flaws and focused on his attributes, what he offered as opposed to what he didn't.

However, it's important to note that the evening could have turned out completely differently, regardless of whether I was in a great mood or whether he was physically my type or not. At any point during the evening, either one of us could have broken the rapport which had been building up. For example, he could have become sulky when other men tried to dance or talk with me; he could have gone too far with his cockiness, and his witty remarks could have slowly turned to insults; he could have flirted with other women; he could have got drunk; he could even have got cold feet and bottled out at the last minute! These are just a few examples of mistakes which could have jeopardised the final outcome.

Instead, however, he took control of the situation. He was the one who had my favourite song played; knowing he was logistically in the great position of knowing the DJ, he took full advantage of the fact. By taking direct action and actively creating a 'moment', he maximised his chances of escalating the interaction. When my song was playing, he kissed me – which was refreshing, because in the past a lot of men I've danced with wanted to kiss me, and the moment had been nothing short of perfect, but in the end they were too scared to make their move.

So, as you can see from this example, every interaction can be broken down and explained in a cold, almost clinical manner, and this is precisely how it should be done. Don't be tempted to recollect your conquests with vague, romanticised ideas of 'love at first sight' or 'uncontrollable chemistry'. These notions, while they might make fantastic material for a Jackie Collins novel and make you feel excited about yourself ('magic' usually does), won't help you in the long run to understand how attraction can be built and replicated.

You must from this moment on learn to become practical. I want you to learn what works and what doesn't; I want you to learn how to read people, how to become free from fear, how to take full advantage of situations or events; I want you to learn how to maximise your chances with *any type of woman*, how to become socially intelligent – and how to produce those fantastic opportunities, rather than waiting for them to happen.

I will teach you the fine art of destroying your 'approach anxiety' with practical techniques, and help you to understand exactly how to create positive circumstances in others with psychological techniques that are tried and tested. I'll also teach you how to study your target and how to understand the importance of logistics, how to master the art of conversation via a practical system to get even the most difficult and/or unresponsive girl to talk to you.

I'll help you to understand the importance of body language and share with you the methods that enable you to perfect it. I'll also illuminate the female mind and hopefully destroy some of the misconceptions men have about women. (Although I will also confirm the assumptions that are true!)

With my help, you will first confront your weaknesses and then destroy them, with the aid of practical systems and techniques. From there you will learn to identify strengths and advantages, and to magnify them until they become larger than life.

So much can be achieved with knowledge and control.

So, no more excuses: take control!

UNDERSTANDING WHAT WOMEN WANT

The man who creates chemistry knows his target inside out.

MY FRIEND ONCE told me the story of a date she went on years ago, with the guy who'd become her long-term boyfriend. It was their fourth date and, after dinner, they decided to walk back to his house for a drink. However, my friend confided in me that, at the time, she still wasn't sure whether she liked him enough to sleep with him, and so she was going over in her head how she could explain to him she wasn't ready without hurting his feelings.

Then, as they walked back to his house, an old woman with a cute dog walked past them. He suddenly stopped walking and let go of my friend's hand, going straight over to the old lady and her dog.

He bent down and began to enthusiastically pat the dog, asking the old lady the dog's name and saying how much he loved that particular breed. The old lady was very happy to tell him her dog's entire life-story, as he politely smiled and listened as he tickled her pet's belly.

Meanwhile, my friend was left standing at the side, watching this adorable interaction between her date and the little animal. After a short time, the date thanked the old lady and went back to my friend as if nothing had happened.

She later revealed to me that this small incident had really touched her, making her see him in a completely new light. As a result – although obviously not entirely due to the dog! – within eight months they were happily living together.

Years later, however, my friend realised one day that she'd never heard her boyfriend mention dogs again after that date. In fact, when they moved in together she had wanted to get a dog, but he said it was, "out of the question!"

"But what about that dog the old lady had, the one you liked so much on one of our early dates?" she asked, obviously confused by his rigid response.

"What dog?" he replied.

She looked at him full of reproach, as he tried desperately to recall what she was talking about. He smiled mischievously when he eventually remembered the old lady and her little dog.

"You bastard!" she snapped, realising how he had fooled her. "You never liked dogs at all!"

"Look," he began, his mischievous smile now turning into laughter, "I know girls love that shit – and it worked, didn't it?"

Because they were now in a proper loving relationship, her anger didn't last long and she began to laugh with him.

In addition, my friend told me he revealed to her that he had a friend who was even more manipulative. Apparently, his friend had an aquarium in his house with cute little goldfish that he'd show whenever he brought a woman back to his flat. (Always making up the fishes' names on the spot!) He boasted that it always seemed to make girls think he was adorable, and that the aquarium had "sealed the deal" plenty of times!

I also personally knew a man who had the whole third series of *Sex and the City* at his home, which he'd purposely put out on display whenever he managed to get a date back to his place (although, of course, he'd never watched it!). He told me that the girls always got excited about the fact that he loved their favourite TV show.

Even Gambler has a little photograph of himself from when he was on vacation in China, a very cute photo of him shaking hands with a small monkey. He says girls always seem to love this picture (I know I do!), and so he purposefully lets them see it whenever they go over to his flat!

Irrespective of whether it's right to play these little games, on some level these men understand what women like. Although some people will think it sneaky and a little unorthodox (including myself), it nevertheless can't be denied that they've studied their target and have used what they learned to help get what they want!

KNOWING YOUR TARGET

Ask yourself the first question of many that I will pose to you in this book: "How much do I know about women?"

Could you write a 700-page book on the psychology of the female mind? Or could you just about muster a page on the subject? Is your knowledge limited to the knowledge and snippets you gained from reading a few issues of *Cosmopolitan*?

When I pose this question to my students, the most common reply I get is the 'rough idea' answer – which usually translates into they've read a book about women at some point, most likely written by a man. Or maybe they have a close friend who happens to be a woman, who gives them vague bits of advice now and again. As a result, they have a 'rough idea' about who women are and what they want.

Now, imagine for a moment that you are in advertising, marketing or sales. (Perhaps you are in this field already, in which case what I'm about to say will come to you as no surprise.)

Imagine that one day your boss asks you to take on a campaign to sell a product – having only a 'rough idea' about your target customer would not only be detrimental but also arrogant. This would be like someone being blindfolded, throwing a dart and merely hoping it'll hit the target because they already have a 'rough idea' where the dartboard is positioned.

Essentially, your familiarity with your target should stretch as far as your resources will allow. If possible, you should know your target so well that you have the ability to predict their reaction with high levels of accuracy. Your familiarity should give you the confidence to know what they want, perhaps even a little more than they do themselves. The aim is to literally know your target inside out.

Now take a moment to imagine that you possessed even half that amount of knowledge and understanding of the average woman; imagine that you could predict many of her responses and reactions, and even match them to your own. Now ask yourself the following question: "If I could know women inside out, what status would that give me in comparison to other men, who are throwing darts blindfolded?" Just think: if you had a vast amount of knowledge on the female mind, on what level would that place you before the interaction had even begun?

I don't claim that this book will teach you how to achieve such a high status, or even that a hundred books could teach you this! But the point is you require some important insights into the average female mind: why she does things that seem out of sync with what she says; why she feels particular emotions in certain situations; why she might desire things that make no sense to the average man. This will help you to understand and familiarise yourself with your target.

FAMILIARITY

After you have read and digested all of the information in this book, the level of familiarity with your target won't end there; in fact, it will begin there. You will continue to study women and you will increase in confidence by being around them a lot more. Make the effort from time to time to read what women read, watch what they watch, find out what interests them and what repels them; you'd be surprised to discover how much you can actually learn about women simply from reading their monthly magazines! Of course, I'm fully aware that men find these magazines boring – what with their lack of sport and the latest recommended upmarket car purchases – but try to read them now and again and you'll be surprised to find how much these magazines talk about male-female relationships and sex – sometimes in very graphic detail!

Read women's literature too – and don't make the mistake of ruling this out by thinking 'chick lit' is some kind of Mills & Boon romantic novel; again, you might actually be surprised at how graphic some of these books can get!

Take the time to watch porn directed by women *for* women. It's now getting easier to find than it used to be, but you still have to search around a bit. Even if you find it a bit dull, you'll still be learning what turns us on both visually and mentally (porn for women directed by women is usually more psychologically erotic than male porn). There is also a lot of erotic fiction out there for women and, even better, a few very good compendiums (which I recommend you read) of women's sexual fantasies.

Watch films that women watch, especially when there is a cast member who women swoon over. Instead of getting sulky and commenting on how he looks like an idiot, or how he'd be rubbish in a fight, take time to see what he's doing which is actually making these women temporarily turn into weak-kneed teenage girls again!

Let the cloak of mystery that women have been shrouded in for so long slip away. Become familiar with women, and change that 'rough idea' of who they are and what they want into a clear vision instead.

There is always a fear of the unknown, so change that right now and get to *know* the unknown.

THE NEED WITHIN

Recently, two dozen women between the ages of 18 and 40, from different backgrounds, were all gathered together. Each woman was asked to take a moment to imagine their ideal man; how he would look, how he would behave, how he would speak, how he would be in bed, what his values and beliefs would be, etc. When the women had this vision clearly in their heads, they were then asked to write a list of ten points which made this man their ideal partner.

Of course, it will come as no surprise to find that, upon first glance, these lists varied from woman to woman, all dependent on a variety of factors such as her upbringing, background, age, personal tastes and personal experiences, etc. For example, while some focused mainly on physical appearance, others seemed to be more interested in personality. First impressions concluded it would be impossible to create one man who'd be able to satisfy all of these different wants and needs. *No wonder men are having such a hard time these days,* I thought. However, it was only when the women were asked to start slowly eliminating points one by one – from ten points to the last remaining two or three – that any kind of pattern began to take shape.

The conclusion was that these women were all ultimately looking for one characteristic – and that characteristic was strength.

So, why was strength the overall defining factor?

When men are asked what they think is the most important quality to be found in a woman, they nearly always agree that it's loyalty; personality traits and other preferences are meaningless in a relationship if there is no loyalty. However, when it came to the women's lists, although loyalty seemed to always be in the top three, strength always seemed to ultimately take precedence.

The man who makes chemistry understands that a woman must respect him before she can be attracted to him.

THE PRIMAL NEED

Here comes the scientific bit.

Scientists and psychologists will say these two separate desires make perfect sense; they are programmed into us from the moment of conception and, although environment and upbringing play a significant part in who we are, in this case nature wins over nurture; the desire for a strong man that lies within a woman is a primal need inherited from her ancestors.

Evolutionary scientists have explained why these two particular needs are still dictating what we search for in an ideal mate today: years before DNA testing was ever available to us, men had to rely solely on their wives' word to guarantee that the child she was carrying was in fact his. Since he could never be 100 per cent sure, her loyalty was paramount.

With women, on the other hand, up to only 100 years or so ago (less than that in some cultures, still true today in the most extreme examples) were forced to rely on the strength of their partner to literally keep them alive. The stronger he was – whether in terms of social influence or physical strength – the higher the status in his tribe or clan. And, by securing such a man as her own, she in turn would be offered protection and respect by others around her.

"But things have changed since then!" I hear you scream. At least for the greater part in industrial societies, I agree this is the case. Women thankfully now have the opportunities to forge their own careers and the right to own their own property and land; they have the option to work in government across most of the world and, as recent history shows, they can even become world leaders. Women can now even have a child without being in any kind of relationship whatsoever. In short, they have the ability to be completely independent and free of men altogether.

So why are most women still opting for strength as the most important factor in their ideal man? Because it is their primal need, the strength of which is so deep-rooted that it cannot change easily.

Maybe in another 20,000 years that same need will have evolved into something else. But for now, at this moment in time, strength is what she wants; it is her need and it should not – and cannot – be ignored.

THE EVER-CHANGING DESIRES

Even with the above knowledge, there is still the temptation for a man to get caught up in her superficial and ever-changing desires. In doing so, both parties ultimately let her caprices take precedence over her primal need.

Such whims are not nearly important enough to stand in your way of getting her. If a girl says she only likes tall guys (a superficial requirement), does that mean she will never go out with a short guy? I personally tend to be more drawn to really funny guys who share my sense of humour, yet I have dated serious men who do not make me laugh and have gone on to have great relationships with them.

There are countless untold people who end up with a partner who was not what they would have described as their 'type', whether this relates to looks or personality. And why? Well, simply because our superficial and ever-changing desires can be shifted and manipulated with great ease.

In order to build up comfort and good rapport in the early stages, it can be beneficial for you to find out what these desires are – but only for the sake of helping you to improve the conversation flow, and to help you connect more easily with her on a surface level.

Understanding and accepting that her primal need is much stronger than her superficial desires (hobbies, interests, political beliefs, etc) will ultimately empower you and separate you from the defeatists – the men who spend their time worrying about whether they are compatible or not, or whether they can fit into her list of superficial ideals. Because of this, they end up giving up as soon as they realise they are not 'her type', or simply because they cannot connect with her on the surface level.

When I was in my teens, I had a passion for 'bad boys', as did a lot of girls around me at the time; we saw them as rebels, dangerous, sexy, unpredictable creatures, and we would sit in fascination as they told us their tales of defiance, of their ability to command respect, their non-conformity and, occasionally, their crimes. I remember how I'd boast to my friends about the amount of times they got in trouble with the police, and of how they were so fearless and carefree.

This lasted until I was around 19 years old but, slowly, via a combination of age, circumstances and experience, I began to tire of the bad boys. It was a gradual transition, but that rebelliousness I was once so attracted to began to seem like it was simply frustration and unspent energy. It demonstrated weakness rather than strength, and the lack of empathy for others became increasingly upsetting – especially when it was in relation to me.

I found myself becoming more attracted to caring men; men who had ambition to create and be successful, rather than self-destructive failures. Equally, however, there are women I know who used to go for the sensitive, quiet guys – the type of guys who would make good marriage material, the ones who were studying to become a doctor or a lawyer, who would remain faithful and keep a roof over their heads for years to come. Yet, after a while, these women began to yearn for more excitement and danger, having become bored with Mr Reliable. After this transition, these women began their search for the rebel, the one who lives from day to day and thinks a pension scheme is something people only think about when they are 80 years old. The mirror inverse of me, these women's superficial desires changed simultaneously, taking a 180-degree turn.

The moral of the story? Men all over the world are getting too caught up with superficial desires that women specify, leaving them both confused and frustrated. What you will discover is not how to be every girl's type – which is a fruitless task and would require you to never actually be yourself – but rather, you will master being the man that all girls want. What she wants is dictated to her by a primal need – and her need is strength.

The strength of who you are.

• STEP THREE •
CONFIDENCE AND THE MISTAKE OF BEING VAGUE

The master seducer understands that he must know his strengths as much as he knows his weaknesses.

JUST BE CONFIDENT

SO NOW YOU know that the woman's key need in a man is strength. But I know that you're now asking, "What type of strength?" or "Strength in what area?"

Strength can be translated as strength of character, self-belief or power, but more often than not it usually means confidence. However, I'm fully aware that saying you must be more confident in your interactions with women is a statement you've already heard time and time again – and have most probably tried, with short-lived success at best.

Let me give you an example: when I first started public speaking, I was really bad. I would stand on the stage and feel my legs begin to wobble and my mind go blank. People would say to me, "Just be more confident," to which I would respond, "But I *am* confident! I'm a confident person who can talk to anyone, and I'm confident in nearly all I do, so stop telling me to just be confident!"

The truth was it had nothing to do with whether I had confidence or not, but more to do with the fact that I wasn't used to public speaking and had not yet developed the required skills necessary.

21

And so, instead of telling myself I simply had no confidence, I decided to take control of the situation; I went to professionals who taught me the techniques and skills needed for public speaking. With a combination of the knowledge I gained and some more practice, I became a good public speaker and now I no longer feel nervous.

If I'd listened to the people who told me to "just be confident", I would have probably started to develop a complex as a result of thinking that I was, in fact, a person without confidence. Instead, I chose to accept that public speaking was a very small part of my life that I had not yet learned to master, and then I went and did something about it.

So if you feel that the fact you're not doing well with women is simply because you have no confidence, then stop right there and start telling yourself that you *are* a confident person who has just not yet learned the requisite skills and techniques. This is exactly what I did with regard to public speaking – and it worked!

As you may have gathered by now, vague advice is strictly off-limits in this book, and telling someone to "just be confident" is an extremely vague – and therefore useless – piece of advice. Many of my students come to me to say that they have no confidence, and maybe you've heard yourself saying the same thing. If this is the case, one way of helping you get away from this negative opinion you may have of yourself is by completing the first of many exercises I'm setting for you.

I want you to write down a list of things you feel confident in doing that have nothing to do with 'pickup' or women. Some of you will already know exactly where your confidence lies; maybe you are someone who has excelled in several aspects of your life. However, confidence can be apparent in some of the most simple day-to-day activities which we take for granted: even the fact that you wake up in the morning and go to work takes a degree of confidence, as does renting or buying a property, driving a car, speaking another language, taking care of a friend or family member when they are unwell, organising a holiday, doing well at work or being good at a hobby – all require confidence.

However small or insignificant it seems, nearly everything we do requires some form of confidence. But, unfortunately, the daily verbal and non-verbal repetition of 'I have no confidence' is literally destroying the confidence that we *do* have.

For your task, write out the list and surprise yourself by seeing how many things you can actually note down. From that moment on, ban the phrase 'I have no confidence' from ever passing your lips again!

PINPOINTING YOUR STICKING POINTS

Hopefully, with this new list in your possession to quietly remind you of your hidden confidence, you will see success with women as just a skill you have not yet learned and so have not yet mastered.

But you will!

So now we move on to the next exercise. Pinpointing your exact problem(s) in relation to women will help put them into perspective. Big, dramatic statements such as, "I'm hopeless with women," or, "I have no confidence when talking to girls," will do nothing but make the situation seem impossible to overcome before you even begin trying! However, by actually pinpointing our problems in any particular part of our life we can make the impossibly large mountain transform into a range of small hills; each one can then receive the attention it requires, and you can work effectively and practically to overcome it.

In this next exercise, you are going to write another list which will specify the exact problems you have with women. (However, be sure to avoid the vague terms 'confidence', 'hopeless' and 'useless'.) To help you get started, here are some of the most common problems that my students experience:

- I feel scared of approaching certain women because I'm afraid they will intimidate me.
- I don't know what to say to her as an opener without it sounding sleazy.
- I don't know what to say to her as an opener at all.
- I run out of material/things to say usually within the first couple of minutes.
- I'm scared of beautiful women as I feel they could never possibly like me, when there are better-looking men than me out there.
- I feel that when she finds out I'm poor or unsuccessful in my current job she will reject me, thus making my insecurities in that area even worse.
- I have had bad experiences with women and do not want to jeopardise the recovery I'm making from the past.
- I cannot escalate the interaction to a more sexual level, in case I ruin the level of connection/interaction I have now. This leads me to becoming just another friend.
- I cannot maintain eye contact because I feel they will see how scared I am during the interaction.
- My hands are all over the place when I'm talking to a woman, and it makes me look like a weirdo.
- I'm scared she will reject me in front of my friends/her friends/other people, and then I won't be able to live it down.
- I can't approach a beautiful/any woman without being drunk, as alcohol makes me feel strong and funny, and without it I'm not.
- I only go to a few places in my area where everyone knows

each other, and if I'm rejected I'll lose a lot of kudos; regulars might notice it, drawing too much attention to me, which will make me even more nervous.

- I have no problem in the approach, but I feel I end up having to qualify myself during the conversation, which upsets me and turns her off.
- I end up making her laugh and this, in turn, makes me become some sort of jester who is only there to amuse her and her friends.
- I seem to end up insulting her or hurting her feelings, when all I was trying to do was be cheeky. So now I feel I'm constantly watching every word that comes out of my mouth, leaving the conversation dull and homogenised.
- I used to be great with women, then I got into a long relationship and my friends have all moved on in that time, leaving me having to play the single game on my own. I seem to have lost all my knowledge and feel ill at ease with women.
- I don't want to come across as desperate.
- I don't want to come across as creepy/pervy.
- I've never had a girlfriend and I know absolutely nothing about women – which makes me feel scared, as if I'm stepping into uncharted territory.
- I end up talking too much.
- I respect women so much that I actually feel guilty when trying to inject sexuality into the interaction.
- I have put on/lost weight recently, and feel I'm very unattractive. I feel women are making up their minds straight away before I even open my mouth.
- Women always tell me I'm too intense and that it intimidates them. But when I try to tone it down I feel like I'm being someone else, and then they say I'm too quiet.

PINPOINTING YOUR STRENGTHS

One of the aspects of my job I enjoy most — apart from 'bitch shields' (Step Ten) – is when I get my students to pinpoint the attributes they already have which will make them good with women. Sometimes, it takes a lot of encouragement, as in a few extreme cases some of my students feel absolutely certain that they have *no redeeming qualities* whatsoever when it comes to women. But, with a little role-play, some off-topic conversation and, of course, my constant attention to detail, I am able to raise their awareness regarding character traits they never realised they had – and which are actually very appealing to women.

For example, some of my students have great body language which they are able to use naturally, and yet they have no idea how appealing it is! Others possess fantastic conversation skills which are absolutely unique and, after our session, they learned how to use them in order to help them attract women. In addition, some of my students were totally unaware that they maintained fantastic eye contact. And, as is often the case, some could be incredibly funny but, unfortunately, their jokes were wasted on a circle of friends who had tired of their wit.

I remember in particular one of my students, called Theo, who was a stickler for good manners. He would hold open the door for me, and make sure any ladies behind me received the same treatment. He would pull back the chair for me, and even stand when I left to go to the restroom; of course, when I came back he'd stand up.

He would insist that, no matter what, he was unprepared to abandon the good manners towards women that was a product of his upbringing.

He battled for a long time with this, believing that having such old-fashioned good manners was the very thing that held him back from being successful with women. Little did Theo know that not only were his manners attractive, and what immediately separated him from the average bad-mannered male, but it was also attractive when he took pride in being a man of good manners. It was only when he started to feel ashamed of his good manners that he became less appealing. It was the strength of his stage (i.e. overall body language and presence – see Step Four) that was letting him down. Not his good manners.

There are so many other examples of my past students, each of whom had more qualities than they realised, and the reason they never realised this was because, unfortunately, they were too focused on the sticking points.

You, like my previous students, might also be totally unaware of the attributes you possess, and it can be hard to recognise them without the help of an honest (preferably female) opinion. In addition, they are also made more difficult to spot if you have been telling yourself for so long that you are hopeless with women and then continue to reconfirm that thought every day of your life, possibly for years, and, as a result, it has literally created an emotional block (where your negative emotions prevent you from being able to clearly see reality). If, on the other hand, you are able to see your positive traits clearly, you should then have no problem with compiling the next list!

For this exercise, I would like you to write down all the strengths you possess in relation to women and, just like the first list, remember to make it as detailed as possible by staying away from vague terminology.

As before, in order to help get you started, below are some of the most common attributes my students feel they have which can help with women:

- I am able to approach women because I have never had a problem approaching strangers.
- I can make women laugh.
- I feel comfortable around the majority of women.
- I have no issues in asking a girl out because I believe you have to be in it to win it.
- I have excellent manners with women, and always treat a woman like a lady.
- I have a lot of female friends, so I understand women probably better than the average man.
- I am great at making conversation with anybody.
- I prefer female company to male company.
- I'm good looking and know that I'm more physically eye-catching than the other men in the room.
- I have a great personality and I'm very successful in life so, ultimately, I know she will be very happy with me once she gets to know me.
- I'm very intelligent.
- I have a lot of empathy, and I am able to understand other people's feelings very well.
- I'm good in bed.

I understand that completing the above two exercises, and having to write down both positive and negative attributes on paper, is not the nicest of activities you could be pursuing during your afternoon off work, but it is important to begin the process by having an actual list of clearly defined points you wish to work on rather than vague and unhelpful statements about yourself. And, irrespective of whether it is in a couple of weeks or six months time, you will be able to refer back to the list to see how you much you have actually conquered in relation to each particular sticking point.

Go back to these two lists every few weeks or so (depending on what your circumstances are and how much time you have to practise), and cross out the points you no longer have. Importantly, you will feel great about yourself each time you pick up that pen and put a big cross through that past sticking point!

Of course, when you have conquered a sticking point and have proudly crossed it out, you should automatically add a new point to your list of strengths.

• STEP FOUR •
THE STAGE

The successful seducer understands that a woman must respect the man first in order to be attracted to him.

WHAT IS THE STAGE?

'THE STAGE' IS a technique I use in order to teach my students how to perfect their body language. I make no bones about the fact that it's a form of behaviour therapy – and I can proudly state that the results experienced by my previous students have been amazing!

As the old aphorism says, our actions shape our beliefs. With this particular technique, not only will you be able to demonstrate perfect body language but you will also be able to alter any negative thought patterns – by firstly altering your actions, instead of the other way around.

Ever heard the theory that if you smile – even though you might not be *feeling* particularly happy – you can find yourself becoming instinctively happier simply because of the alteration to your facial expression? Or have you ever experienced one of those moments when you're feeling particularly self-conscious or nervous, and you unfortunately have to walk into a crowded room in this less-than-positive frame of mind? But, instead of looking at the floor and shuffling past, what if you opt to walk in with your head held high, wearing a confident smile? As a result, you can't help but notice that the nerves you'd been experiencing just a flicker of a moment before seem to decrease far quicker than you thought they might, simply because of the way you carried yourself and the alteration in your body language.

These are classic examples of the behavioural therapy that forms the basis of this chapter.

I want you to imagine that there are two types of stages from which we always perform: the Weak Stage and the Strong Stage. Obviously, since you now know the woman's ultimate need from a man is strength, it comes as no surprise that you'll be aspiring toward the latter.

The stage is always held up by six columns, each of which represents a point of body language that you will learn how to master in order to create the overall affect of a stronger, and thus more appealing, persona (this is your Strong Stage). Once taught, I will refer back to the stage time and again throughout this book; when you have perfected your own stage, you too will refer to it mentally in all of your interactions with women, and will be constantly aware of the power it possesses.

Eventually, the stage will become an automatic reflex.

THE WEAK STAGE

Imagine that you are constantly interacting with others whilst standing on a stage. Unfortunately, that stage is sometimes very weak; it feels fragile, almost as if it will cave in at any given moment. The columns which support the stage are made of paperclips and you can almost feel it creaking and wobbling. As a result, you feel at your most vulnerable and unsure.

Some people will be aware of their stage being particularly weak when talking to certain people in authority. Some feel it with people they regard as of higher status than themselves. Some experience the Weak Stage during some form of public speaking (as I used to!). It happens to others when talking to a new group of people they are unfamiliar with, or regard as more intelligent than themselves, or more aggressive, or cooler. Some people experience the Weak Stage during a job interview, or in any situation where they believe they are being assessed in some way.

However, in your case this particular Weak Stage rears its ugly head during an interaction with a particular woman – irrespective of whether she's a woman you're approaching randomly, a woman to whom you're attracted, an Alpha woman, one of a group of women, or even all women in general!

When this happens, all the negative thoughts come flooding back. It's an all-too-familiar scenario to some people, who might then automatically take a drink to deaden the feelings that arise from their negative thoughts. When these thoughts enter your head, you might find that your hands start fidgeting, you begin tapping your fingers or twiddling your thumbs; your eye contact might start shifting crazily from one place to the next; your vocal tone might become weaker than normal; your facial expression might tell a thousand tales that you wish were suppressed. With so much subconsciously going on in the space of just a few moments, you may be completely aware that your legs keep shifting your weight from side to side, or your arms seem to have become two awkward, uncontrolled parts of your body. (Either that or they're surgically stuck to your side, unable to move!) And then, at the end of this exhausting, weakening, self-chastising moment, your mind goes completely blank, your stage caves in and it's game-over.

THE STRONG STAGE

And then, even when all might seem lost, there are the times when your stage is strong; those rare (at least so far) moments when it feels as it's made of solid oak, with each column of the strongest marble that even an earthquake couldn't shift.

This stage often supports our weight effortlessly when we're talking with the people we are close to, such as friends or family members. It can also magically construct itself when you speak to people that you feel are of lesser status than you, either because they are of a lower intellect, lower class or occupy a lower position at your workplace. It might appear in certain unexpected situations when others are revealed as having a very weak stage, perhaps in public speaking or performing. Perhaps your stage is strong when talking to women you are not attracted to – or women you *are* attracted to, but who you've been introduced to via friends, making the situation easier. But, irrespective of the circumstances when your Strong Stage appears, you will notice that both your interaction and your body language are strong.

For instance, you will find that your legs are in a naturally Alpha stance (whether sitting or standing); your arms are not an awkward mess, but are tools that assist your hands in making confident gestures; your eye contact is relaxed, and your facial expression controlled and warm; your smile is genuinely welcoming rather than forced, you might even be grinning like a Cheshire cat! In addition, you will notice that your vocal tone exudes self-assurance, and is timed to a perfect rhythm rather than sounding – and feeling – rushed. And later, the next time you're on that Strong Stage, you will notice once again that all your actions are controlled and confident.

THE SIX COLUMNS OF YOUR STAGE

The six columns which hold up that all-important stage must correspond directly with the six most important aspects of body language. They are:

- Leg position
- Arm position (and movement)
- Hand gestures
- Eye contact
- Facial expression
- Vocal tone

Each of these points of body language (the 'stage columns') must be strengthened until they are collectively capable of holding up the stage on which you stand and speak from. They should enable you to go into any interaction without being fearful of anything – with any number of women, using any approach (ranging from the shy guy to the Alpha male, from the attractive to the intimidating man), and in any situation, day or night, regardless of whether it's in a coffee shop or a club, without ever feeling intimidated, nervous, shy or awkward.

Remember:
The columns = each individual point of body language.
The stage = the end result/your overall body language.

FIRST COLUMN: LEG POSITION

When standing, your legs should be fairly far apart – not so far that you look as if you're about to do the splits but, as a general rule, it's best to keep them the same distance apart as the width of your shoulders. This will stop you from giving into the temptation of shifting your weight from side to side, which signals to the girl that you're uncomfortable. Similarly, if your legs are too close together, it also can make your stance seem more like that of an unsure or nervous male. Once your legs are positioned apart correctly, imagine your feet are grounded so firmly that anyone who might push into you by accident will be unable to shift your balance.

Sitting down, your legs should also be apart, with one leg close into the chair and the other stretched out in front of you, creating an asymmetrical look. When they are at clubs, many of the pickup artists I work with are constantly asked – by men as well as women – if they are the manager, or sometimes even the owner. The key reason for this is because of they way they sit. They are usually stretched out, with some even taking it to the extent that they are practically lying down on the sofa as if about to go to sleep. (Although you clearly need a strong stage all round to pull this one off!) It goes to show how much power we can make the people around us perceive that we have, just by the way we sit or stand.

Good body language - Alpha stance.

Bad body language.

SECOND COLUMN: ARMS

The arms are by far the most awkward part of the anatomy; they are much more noticeable than the legs and, of course, what we do with our arms affects what we do with our hands too.

Very often, when you go into a bar or club and see a man talking to a woman, you can instantly spot the level of his comfort just by watching his arms; for example, sometimes you can spot when they seem to be surgically sewn to the side of his torso, which makes him look nervous and/or scared. Obviously his comfort level is noticeably low.

The other notable signs relate to nervousness, when his arms are doing the complete opposite – flapping around all over the place – which is indicative of the fact that he's either trying way too hard to be some sort of court jester or, even worse, that he's drunk!

If you come across like any of these examples, then a great way to fix it is to keep one arm to the side, with the other left loose to enable you to make freer gestures. When you've chosen the arm you wish to keep by your side, simply put the thumb into the hook of your jeans or your pocket. But please note: it's important that you don't put the whole of your hand in your pocket, as this can make you look like a naughty schoolboy in the process of being told off by his teacher! In addition, it can also be very tempting to start playing with that loose change in your pocket – and girls hate that!

Below are two illustrations to help make this clear: the first shows incorrect body language in relation to the arms; the second shows a more desirable positioning of the arms and legs when standing.

Bad body language.

Good body language.

Making a habit of the above position will also help you control your hands a lot better. For example, imagine if you have one hand firmly in place and only the other one is allowed to gesture; the temptation of twiddling thumbs, rubbing your hands together – or making any other nervous gesture! – is therefore immediately eliminated.

THIRD COLUMN: HANDS

When you wish to make a point, or become more animated in your interaction, you'll be naturally inclined toward making gestures. However, because you've adopted a new arm position (see previous image above), your gestures will be made with only one hand.

There are plenty of gestures you can make, such as pointing to yourself or – even better – touching your chest when referring to yourself. You can also push your hand in a downwards motion when making a point (with palms facing the floor).

If you want to point to her, rather than using your finger in the accusatory manner, you can either use your hand, palm facing her or palm facing you, and simply move the hand in her direction, but make sure this is not face level or breast level; keep it more to her stomach. Often, men make the mistake of getting dangerously close to a woman's breasts when gesturing, which consequently makes the girl feel extremely vulnerable. In order to avoid this issue altogether, be sure to respect her space.

There are plenty of hand gestures which, if made correctly, will help maximise your overall body language. However, there is one gesture I will warn you to stay away from, which a lot of men use when they feel shy or nervous. I call it 'palms facing heaven for help'.

Let me explain: your hand(s) should never be turned palms facing upward toward the sky, yet this is a common mistake made by a lot of people. When someone is talking and simultaneously using the 'palms facing heaven for help' gesture, it says they are unsure of what they are saying. By holding your hands up in this way, it can also send a subliminal message to the girl that you need help. Look at the image on the next page to see what I mean.

Imagine you speak to a girl and she asks you about your job. When you begin to explain, if you use this particular gesture she'll subconsciously think that you feel unsure that your job is good enough to impress her, or that you need her help or validation to continue. Of course, this is not the impression you want to give, so avoid!

Bad hand gestures.

Important note: there are plenty of men who use both hands when gesturing and have no problems when doing so. However, if you are like many men who feel their hands are a hindrance rather than an aid (be honest!), then simply keep one arm motionless and the thumb of that arm hooked in your trouser pocket or belt (as described above), in order to avoid nervous reflexes such as picking at your fingers (not the most attractive habit!), twiddling your thumbs or rubbing your hands together. Start slowly with one hand and then, within time, you'll progress to using both.

FOURTH COLUMN: EYE CONTACT

Non-verbal forms of communication often equal our ability to verbally express a thought. We are less aware of our non-verbal communication skills like body language and – especially – eye contact, yet they often speak louder than our words.

When you maintain eye contact, you present an air of confidence in yourself and trust in what you're communicating. People who listen to what you are saying will take you more seriously, and will take what you say as important. However, failing to maintain eye contact during a conversation can send mixed signals, often construed as a tell-tale sign that you may not be 100 per cent truthful with what you're saying. Liars tend not to keep eye contact. However, if the lack of eye contact is not perceived as an indicator of lying, then the person may be seen as trying to conceal a lack of interest, or as possessing a short attention span.

With that said, don't feel that breaking eye contact is an absolute sin! It is, of course, permissible to drop eye contact for a moment or two, but this depends more on the timing and the manner in which you break it. For instance, never break eye contact when you are at the sexual escalation stage (e.g. the point when you're close to kissing her), or when you're telling her how you feel. Furthermore, if you say anything that's considered to be strong or intense, or has the ability to shift the mood, then you must make doubly sure that you hold eye contact – otherwise you could come across as a man who can talk the talk but not walk the walk.

Importantly, when you do break eye contact, make sure your eyes break away to the side, never upwards or downwards; breaking eye contact upwards can give the impression that you're either lying or you're bored. I'm aware that us ladies sometimes break our eye contact and move our eyes towards the floor, but we do this intentionally and the result can be endearing. (We often do this to show a certain playful bashfulness, which is one of the little weapons we use to make you guys melt – we know our power!)

However, if a man were to do this it wouldn't create the same effect, but would instead imply uncertainty and inexperience.

Note that if a man wants to play the 'cute card', he has to be less than 20 years old – it won't work beyond this age! However, even if you *are* this age, it can still lead to the dreaded 'let's just be friends' scenario. And remember – you won't be 20 forever!

So remember, when you want to break eye contact, make sure of the following:

- Break it to the side, not upward or downward.
- Do not break it when you have just said – or are in the process of saying – something important, or something which has the ability to create a shift in mood.
- Do not hold her gaze too intensely all the time.
- If she is talking to you about something very important, you should not choose that moment to break eye contact.
- If she says something bitchy or insulting to you, then make sure that you *do not* break eye contact at all, under any circumstances!

Remember, however, that this is not a staring competition, and there is always the possibility that your eye contact can become intimidating!

I remember one wannabe pickup artist who thought he was really good, trying to chat me up in a club. He was a nice looking guy and had fairly good conversation skills and body language, but his eyes were constantly staring into me. It was actually frightening, like he was possessed! As a result, he came across like some total weirdo.

"Who the fuck taught you to do that?" I interrupted him in mid-sentence.

"What?" he replied in complete bewilderment.

"That strange eye thing you've got going on there," I said without holding back.

It came as no surprise when he told me the name of the trainer who'd taught him. I'd met this particular trainer before and noticed that he also seemed to have a real staring problem, somehow under the illusion that it was really good to keep eye contact with a girl the entire time. The problem with this was that he was teaching others to do it too! The wannabe pickup artist eventually became my student and, since that time, I've taught him how to use eye contact correctly. He now does much better with women!

In order for you to ensure that your eye contact doesn't come across too intensely, think of how you behave when you speak to people you know well. The next time you speak with them, intentionally take note of what you're doing with your eyes; this behaviour should be transferred to your future interactions with women.

FIFTH COLUMN: FACIAL EXPRESSION

One must always be aware of one's facial expressions. Commonly, once people have mastered their hand gestures, they unfortunately tend to let their suppressed nerves show on their face. However, over time I've noticed that people who are constantly in the media spotlight are masters of controlling this problem – and we can learn from them.

If you observe a full-blown celebrity before they were truly famous by watching their early TV interviews, compare them to their more recent appearances. You'll see that their facial expressions in the earlier interviews are far less controlled. They probably revealed their true emotions when asked difficult questions or when put in an awkward position by the interviewer, and the viewer may have been adept in picking up on their nerves. It might make the celebrity seem more familiar and 'average' to the viewer, but also unsure and awkward. It gave both the interviewer and you at home – watching from the comfort of your living room, possibly mocking the interviewee's nerves and slip-ups – the chance to feel superior to the star onscreen.

Of course, as time goes on the celebrity has the opportunity to replay the interviews and is then forced to confront all of their uncontrolled and unwanted expressions or behaviours. With the benefit of this hindsight and their surrounding managers, PR executives, etc, the celebrity subsequently becomes more aware of themselves and of the media glare. They learn how to quickly take control before anyone else has the chance to notice.

You and all the other non-celebrities on this planet are not given the opportunity to come face-to-face with your mistakes. Unlike the celebrity, you (unfortunately) have no agent or manager to constantly remind you; if this were the case, then you could make the necessary adjustments so that – at least some of the time – you would come across flawlessly.

Unlike the hand gestures, we are unable to see what our face is doing. It's often a difficult area to tackle, but during our sessions I'm constantly pointing out every unwanted and unintended facial expression that subconsciously sneaks through my students' bravado. Of course, after their absent-minded ways are pointed out, they manage to correct the issue – but only in the short term, undoubtedly due to the fact that I temporarily become the celebrity's manager, a constant and at times annoying reminder of their errors. But, even after a week, they often come back with the same old uncontrolled expressions!

Of course, it takes a long time to forcefully remove old habits and to gain control of those all-important 'nano-expressions', which seem to occur whenever we feel that we've been put on the spot during a conversation. Eventually, however, like most of my students, your facial expressions will become more controlled as your nervousness decreases (the natural result of the improvements you'll be making in other areas of your game).

But, for the time being, you must first make a constant conscious effort to be more aware of your expression when interacting with a woman whom you wish to build chemistry with. For example, make sure that whatever she says or whatever position she tries to put you in, you remain controlled. Regardless of whatever nervous reactions are going on inside your head, you should not show a single one of them through unintended or uncontrolled facial expressions.

Below are two illustrations to help make the point. The first shows the undesirable result of when a man has not perfected his eye contact and facial expression; the second is the desired result.

Needy/uncomfortable facial expression.

Confident facial expression.

THE NERVOUS LAUGH

This point corresponds with the 'facial expressions column' in that it's another extreme reaction. When someone becomes scared or anxious, they believe that at that exact moment a laugh will help mask their true state. But, in actual fact, it only succeeds in highlighting the problem, making the situation even more obvious to the people around them. This must be avoided at all costs!

Once a man gives a nervous laugh to a woman, he literally hands her all the power. As a result, his stage becomes weaker and he becomes less attractive. For example, I had a student called Baz who brought a Dictaphone to record the session. During the lesson, I asked him whether he was aware how often he gave a nervous laugh.

"Do I?" he asked, completely shocked but giggling again.

I told him to listen back to the tape when he got home and to look out for it. (Although he wouldn't have been able to miss it!)

That very evening, Baz wrote me an email telling me how he couldn't believe just how much he was giggling on the recording. Every time there was a silence he would feel the need to fill it with a laugh. In addition, nearly every time he said something he'd need to laugh at the end, thus making it seem like either he wasn't serious or else that he was uncomfortable with what he was saying!

The nervous laugh can become a terrible habit which literally becomes an unwanted reflex, almost like a nervous twitch. Note that it *can*, however, be very cute on a woman, which allows the man a brief moment to see a more vulnerable side to her personality. (Vulnerability is another trait that women like to play on sometimes.) But, as with looking down to the floor, a man behaving like this can create a very unattractive impression. Remember: vulnerability is a trait that men should stay well clear of in the early stages of the interaction.

Playing the vulnerable card – which I know some men do – can have very successful results, but this is an advanced form of pickup and will only work if it's been done intentionally. However, with that said, do not even attempt this until you have learned how to perfect your stage beforehand!

Remember that women want strength and it is, of course, a universally recognised fact that vulnerability is considered a weakness – so keep it out of the interaction!

SYMPATHY FUCKS DON'T REALLY HAPPEN!

SIXTH COLUMN: VOCAL TONE

So now we reach the sixth and final column: vocal tone. It is extremely important that you master this, not only to help all your future interactions with women but with everybody else too.

The way you execute your words can completely change the tone of a conversation; it can alter the mood and create instant shifts in people's perceptions of you. The way you use your voice is very important in every aspect of the interaction, right from the opener to the few moments before you kiss her. And, despite the importance of this element, there are three very common mistakes that men make in relation to their vocal tone, which usually come about when they start to feel nervous or under pressure.

The first mistake is what some trainers like to call 'the hanging *or*'. It describes a man who asks questions which trail off with 'or . . . ?' Example: "Do you like James Bond movies or . . . ?" This incomplete question shows his lack of certainty in what he's asking, and when he uses this lazy way of finishing off what he's saying he also invites her to finish off the sentence for him.

Imagine you are approaching a woman. It's gone smoothly so far, she seems pretty friendly and you start chatting with her. You then begin to ask her a few questions but, unfortunately, for whatever reason you begin to get nervous. And that is when you make the mistake of asking her something like, "So, do you like travelling or . . . uh . . ." As a result of this, you give the impression that you're running out of things to say and also struggling to keep the conversation flowing. Is she boring? Does she not inspire you to want to get to know her? Of course that's not the case, but you need to make sure *she* knows that.

Rather than beginning your question with the less-than-inspirational, 'So . . .' and ending it with the equally flat '. . . or,' it's far better to execute your question almost like a statement; this simple alteration will automatically make you appear a lot more comfortable with the conversation and give the impression that you're confident with where it's going. It also makes you appear less anxious about making such an effort to create a good impression, thus coming across as less needy.

So get rid of that 'So . . .' at the beginning of your question and lose that '. . . or' at the end!

The second common error is when a man lets his sentences trail off into a mumble; this can have a similar effect to the above, making him seem unsure of what he's saying or perhaps even embarrassed. If he finishes off like this he'll be openly inviting the woman to take the lead and finish off his sentences for him. By allowing her to do this, he will subsequently weaken his position in the interaction. Make sure that you *never* allow your sentence to trail off!

The third and most common error is when men let the tone of their sentences rise upwards at the end, finishing off in a question-like style. This should be avoided even when he is actually asking a question. The result of this will make the man seem needy, an unsure little boy asking an adult for permission. In order to avoid this, make sure that your questions come across as statements: don't let your voice trail up at the end of your questions in a needy manner! Apply this technique when you are answering her question too.

In my experience, I've found that a lot of men who feel either nervous or under pressure let their voice trail upwards in a question-like manner, even when they're simply answering her questions. It makes them sound like they're worried whether they can give the right answer or not, like an approval seeker.

Instead, in the future, if she asks you something like, "What do you do?", "What's your favourite film?" or, "Where do you like to go on holiday in the summer?", then make sure your answer is delivered as a statement. Maybe you're wondering what the big deal is, but uncertainty allows her to feel superior to you and it will ultimately turn her off!

Think about it for a moment: if you're answering her questions in that way it's as if you're literally asking her if your chosen answer is acceptable. And FYI: no woman wants to date a man who can't even show certainty or security in his chosen answers, particularly when they relate to himself. Women find it a complete turn-off when a man subconsciously asks her to be the judge of who he is!

Do not allow your stage to collapse because of your vocal tone. It should remain authoritative, yet not intimidating or aggressive. When teaching my students about the importance of vocal tone, they usually presume this means being either louder or deeper or both. But as you now know, focusing on how your sentences and even your questions are delivered plays a far greater role than the resonance of your voice. So be aware of the three common mistakes that you might be making.

SUMMARY OF THE STAGE

Here is an example of how one of my students perfected his stage. In his case he worked especially hard with his particular weak column, which was his vocal tone.

I had a few students who were fairly embarrassed by their line of work; it wasn't that they hated or didn't enjoy their chosen career, they just thought it was a bit of a conversation-killer and that it was considered by most women to be boring. (Once again, this is an example of getting caught up in her superficial desires.)

Let's take Robert, for example. He was a student I coached for only a few sessions. He was a great guy and was one of my favourite students; 28 years old, funny, spoke four languages and worked as a computer software programmer.

When I watched his interactions with women, I was pleased to see that they would respond fairly well to him in those testy early stages; he was always able to execute his openers well, his stage was strong and his image was maximised to the best of his ability. He also used the conversation skills that I had I taught him well and, as a result, was able to connect on hook points – conversation points that can hook her in – and build rapport very quickly.

On one particular occasion, Robert managed to isolate one of the girls that he liked from her group of friends. All was going very well but, as soon as she asked the inevitable question – "So, what do you do?" – his stage collapsed.

When I say this, don't take it to mean that he fell on the floor or began stuttering uncontrollably as if he was having a seizure; it means that the largely successful body language he had perfected began to get noticeably weaker, mainly due to his eye contact and especially his vocal tone.

Importantly, when someone's stage becomes weaker others can notice it in a great many different ways; the nerves can find an outlet via any of the six columns (points of body language). In Robert's case, he looked away for a little longer than necessary, paused a little longer than he needed to and, when he eventually answered her question, his voice trailed off into a mumble. Two of his previously strong, carefully mounted columns – his eye contact and his vocal tone – had begun to weaken.

Here is how the conversation went:

"So, what do you do?" she asked.

He paused, looked away for a second. "I'm a computer software programmer," he answered, his voice trailing off.

Another pause followed, before she sympathetically responded. "That's . . . uh . . . nice."

"Yeah . . ." he replied, followed by another deafening silence.

"So, what do you do?" he asked in turn (his voice rising upwards like that 'unsure little boy' earlier in the chapter), swiftly trying to change the subject.

But, unfortunately for Robert, it was too late. He'd ruined all his hard work simply because he showed a fundamental flaw – that he was somewhat embarrassed about what he did for a living, an impression given through his bad eye contact and poor vocal tone.

What we do for a living is a huge part of our everyday lives and is obviously important – but how we feel about what we do is even more important.

Afterwards, I asked Robert if he hated his job. He laughed at my question and told me that it was quite the opposite, that in actual fact he loved his job. He told me proudly that he chose what hours he could work, earned a lot of money and loved computers. It soon became apparent to me that the problem was not Robert's job, but his fear of her reaction when he told her what it was; he felt that women would be turned off if they knew what he did, or that it would kill the conversation.

To help Robert understand that this was simply a case of getting caught up in her superficial/ever-changing desires, I told him about a man I knew (and still do) who was living at home with his parents. He was also unemployed and claiming benefits off the state. But, because he never had an issue with it and because he never gave a shit whether the girl disapproved of his parasitic mode of income, he always seemed to attract women simply because of the unapologetic manner of who he was and what he did. (Imagine how many more women this guy could have got if he actually had an amazing career!) Robert took this story on board and understood the message clearly.

Later on that evening, Robert had a similar encounter with another woman, but this time he changed things around when it came to answering that inevitable question.

"I'm a computer software programmer," he answered in an unapologetic manner this time around, keeping his eyes firmly connected to hers.

"That's, uh . . . nice," she responded dismissively.

"If it was just nice I don't think I'd be doing it," Robert smiled, still holding strong eye contact.

"Excuse me?"

"Well, would you do a job every day that you thought was just 'nice'?" he asked earnestly.

By turning the question back on her like this, Robert was telling her that he would find it a slight turn-off if a woman was doing a job that she didn't love or wasn't passionate about – but without actually having to say it.

"No, I don't think so," she said, no doubt beginning to question herself as to whether she loved her own job or not.

"Exactly, neither would I," he smiled again.

"So, you like fixing computers?" she responded with a badly thought-out question.

He paused and looked at her quizzically, as if she was a little lost. "I think you'll find that's what a computer technician does, not what I do," he said helpfully.

"Oh, I'm sorry," she said, "I'm not sure if I know what the difference is!" He suddenly had her admitting her own ignorance!

"That's fine, a lot of people don't," he smiled reassuringly. "I'll explain later what it's about."

The conversation was now taking a turn where Robert was showing he'd forgiven her mistake. After this point, he continued to lead the conversation with a level of authority on his side.

This is a great example of someone making sure their stage is strong and, in doing so, altering the outcome of what could have been yet another fruitless interaction. Robert dealt with the situation in a way that, although it seems fantastically simple, in fact employed a system that worked on multiple levels of her mind. Firstly, he managed to maintain pride in his work without overselling his job (which some men do, which is just as bad!) by simply maintaining his strong vocal tone and strong eye contact. Secondly, he managed to switch her gratuitous comments around full circle; she'd tried to make him feel inadequate but, in the end, he turned those tactics around on her, which is far better than if he'd left her feeling superior.

Later on in the interaction, the woman actually began asking him questions about his job and started sharing his enthusiasm. At this point, she also felt she had to compensate by explaining how she loved her work too; in other words, she began qualifying herself to him.

During this interaction, Robert had taken control of both his own reactions and responses and the woman's too. But, most importantly, that night he made sure he had total control over his nerves, not by trying in vain to calm himself or by inwardly telling himself what a great person he was, but by actively strengthening all the columns of his stage – particularly his two weakest points, eye contact and vocal tone.

Robert made sure that not one of the columns would collapse – no matter how difficult it got.

The moral of the story: perfect your stage! Be able to pinpoint which column (point of body language) begins to shake and let you down whenever you feel pressure or nerves. Whether it's your hands which start fidgeting or your eye contact becoming weak, alter it to how it should be straight away.

When your stage is strong, your nerves will diminish

Always remember, our actions shape our beliefs.

A Strong Stage = Strength.

THE THREE ELEMENTS OF ATTRACTION

The man who makes chemistry is in control, makes impact and connects.

WHEN MEN FIND *out what I do, they usually always ask me about the 'special ingredients' needed in order to attract women. This happened recently at a dinner party. The eyes of the man next to me almost popped out of his head with excitement when he found out my area of expertise.*

"So tell me," he said, moving closer to the edge of his chair, "what are the ingredients a man needs to get women?"

Being a naturally difficult woman, I always turn this particular question back onto the questioner. So I smiled, and asked him what he thought the ingredients were.

He thought for a moment, and then gave a list similar to that of most men: "Good looks, confidence, money and the ability to make a woman laugh."

In this instance a man being well endowed wasn't added to the list, although a lot of men do actually think this. But irrespective of all this, why, I asked him – assuming these are indeed the ingredients needed to attract women – are there so many financially poor and physically unattractive men out there getting laid on a regular basis?

He thought for a moment, and then said, "That's true! My

friend Billy is really ugly and hasn't got a penny to his name, yet he gets to shag absolutely gorgeous women!"

"Are you better looking and richer than Billy?" I asked him.

"Definitely," he boasted.

"And are you sleeping with as many women as he is?" I smiled.

"No," he answered, looking to the floor, his ego immediately deflated like a punctured tyre.

I put my hand on his arm and leaned in closer, as if it to share with him the secret he had been hankering for since he was an adolescent. "There are no ingredients," I whispered.

He looked at me like a little boy who had just been told that Father Christmas isn't real.

I continued. "Ingredients are superficial desires that a woman might have, that differ from one woman to the next. It's far better to learn the formula of attraction which, unlike ingredients, does not differ from woman to woman."

The poor thing looked a little confused. Of course, like every other man who had ever posed this question, he was expecting the quick-fix solution to his problems with the ladies.

"Would you like to know the formula of attraction?" I asked him, peering into his confused eyes.

"Will it attract even a really stunning model?" he asked like an excited child.

"The formula works universally," I replied. (I love adding dramatic tension at these moments!)

THE FORMULA OF ATTRACTION

I want to share with you the three vital elements needed for you to build attraction with a woman. These three elements are:

- Control

- Impact
- Connection

The order of these elements is not random but deliberate; each one is a step, starting with control and ending with connection. In this chapter I will break down and explain each element, why they are so important and why they occur in that particular order.

And always remember:

The master seducer takes control in order to create impact, and as a result of making impact he builds a connection.

CONTROL

You are already aware of the absolute necessity of this, as I've deliberately stressed the importance of control at every step of the way so far. If you have not yet fathomed how important control is in picking up the girl you want at the time that you want her, then you need to go back to the beginning and start reading this book again!

Without control, you will be unable to achieve the other two elements needed when building up attraction. Unintentionally, and to some degree subconsciously, control begins before you even say one word to a woman; it begins from the moment you make the decision to approach her and continues all the way up to the point you make the move to kiss her.

In order to maximise your chances of building up attraction with a woman, you will first need to take control of each of the following:

- **Your state of mind in the pre-approach stage.**

- Your body language.
- Your appearance (fashion/haircut/weight).
- Your conversation skills.
- Any point in an interaction where you wish to take it to the next level.
- Your reaction to her responses and your responses to her reactions, both externally and internally.

EXCUSES, EXCUSES

Taking control also means never having to make excuses again! I find men who lack control in this game seem to be the ones with the most excuses. Even if they do muster enough desire to go and talk to a woman, but are then consequently unable to build attraction with her, they will go on to make even more excuses – ultimately pinning the blame on the woman. Excuses such as:

- She was unresponsive.
- She was too shy.
- She was bitchy.
- She didn't make any effort.
- She was in a bad mood.
- She didn't respond the way I thought she would.

These men don't realise they're making excuses which will ultimately hold them back from becoming any good at seduction. They are blaming things on the woman which they actually have the power to change themselves! And that's the great thing about a pickup artist or a natural – they simply don't see any obstacles or challenges which can't be overcome; in fact, they often relish the challenges that 'difficult' women or situations might present them with.

Importantly, taking control is also about taking full responsibility – not only for your successful interactions but also for your failed ones. By taking full responsibility, you will be able to recognise what you have to do the next time you face a similar situation. You'll always gain something useful from each and every interaction, regardless of how long it lasts or how successful it was.

For instance, let's say you go to speak to a shy girl and you are unsuccessful in getting her to open up, which is often the case with introverts. After you leave the interaction, instead of taking the easy option of simply blaming the girl you must instead take responsibility and blame yourself. I understand that this is the last thing you want to do at that moment – but this will enable you to understand that you have the power to change and control the outcome of any interaction, and it will also enable you to gain enough insight to pinpoint the precise moment *when* it went pear-shaped, *why* it went that way and, most importantly, *how* it can be prevented from happening again in the future.

As soon as you understand that taking full responsibility for your interactions is the key to mastering the art of control, from that moment on, each time you speak to another 'difficult' girl you will become more aware of what works and what doesn't. Armed with the experience and knowledge that you gather after each interaction, you will notice that each time you speak to a girl of *any* nature that you might have struggled with before (Alpha women, shy girls, aggressive girls, etc), it will become noticeably easier and your success rate with that particular type of girl will greatly increase. This, of course, will also help you destroy any 'approach anxiety' you might have left.

Excuses are especially popular when men see beautiful women. You should strive to start approaching the most stunning woman in the room, and not be like all the other men who are too busy creating reasons not to speak to her. There are some very common excuses not to talk to beautiful women, such as:

- She's probably a bitch.
- She probably only dates rich sugar daddies.
- She probably only likes really good-looking men.
- I don't have anything to say to her.
- She's probably been approached a hundred times tonight.
- I haven't had enough to drink yet.

Whilst we are on this point, I want to let you in on a little fact that might surprise you: all my stunning friends complain to me that men just stare at them, and by the time those men actually pluck up the courage to go talk to them they've unfortunately drunk way too much; whereas my more 'average-looking' friends do not seem to have these same problems. Presuming a beautiful woman is hassled all the time is a myth. She is usually ogled and stared at, but is approached no more so than any other woman (sometimes even less).

Do not waste time standing around with the 'excuses, excuses' crowd. Instead, choose the better route and separate yourself from these men and their defeatist attitudes. Take control, approach that stunning woman! Remember that, when other women see you approaching the most beautiful woman in the room (and women are fully aware who the most beautiful women are in any venue), you'll instantly display your high standards and high value for all to see.

It is important to realise that, *even if it fails*, rather than getting angry with yourself and with the woman in question, you must instead consider this failed interaction – and all the other failed interactions you might experience – as simply being an opportunity to understanding your weaknesses and sticking points. This will give you the chance to fix them in preparation for the next interaction.

Remember: practice makes perfect. There is no better way to learn how to attract women than actually practising! In addition, theory will remain only theory if not put into practice. As long as you maintain control (it's that word again!) of your emotional reactions, you will begin to see each 'failure' purely as a learning experience which you need to go through in order to perfect your skills; then, in time, those less successful interactions will become less frequent and in turn your rate of successful interactions will start to increase.

Ask yourself this question: do you think that the successful pickup artists out there – such as Gambler – simply read a book one day, went to sleep and that somehow, during the night, all the wisdom from that book was magically absorbed into their system? Do you believe that the next evening, when they went out, they found as if by magic that they were automatically attracting beautiful women and having threesomes with supermodels?

The truth is, they read books; they attended workshops or classes or seminars; then they went out and put what they had learned into practice.

And of course they got blown out! Of course they got rejected! They probably even got into arguments with the meathead boyfriends of girls they were practising on. But, as time went on, they also noticed at some point that they were starting to measure their success rate rather than their failure rate. These pickup artists had to learn how to attract beautiful women the hard way but, nonetheless, they took control of a part of their life they were unhappy with and turned it around, going from one extreme to the other in some cases.

These are the aspects they took control of:

- How to deal with their early rejections, and how it would affect them both emotionally and psychologically.
- Their state of mind every day/evening before they went out to practise.
- The way they looked and how they presented themselves.
- The inclination to blame the woman if they had not managed to build an attraction with her; instead they blamed themselves and, by doing that, recognised what went wrong and fixed it in time for the next interaction.

Ask any of them, "Was it worth it?" and their answer will *always* be, "Yes!"

Let me emphasise the point further: take something you're good at – whether it's driving, computer games or football, etc – but preferably also something you experienced failure with early on, and apply this simple logic to your skills with women. For example, you couldn't always drive, you were not born with the ability; inevitably, you stalled the car, selected the wrong gear and lurched from time to time. Isn't that a part of the process? Skills need to be learned and then polished and perfected; they do not come without a thorough grounding in theory and plenty of practice!

Just remember: by taking control, you will be able to start fulfilling the second vital element of pickup – impact.

IMPACT

The successful seducer understands that being great with women is not about being the funniest man in the room or the best looking, but about offering the alternative.

Once you have mastered control, impact will follow almost naturally. In fact, even the way you hold yourself in comparison to other guys at the bar will now be creating impact. You will notice that girls are more aware of your presence now that you've perfected your stage (taken control of your body language). As a result, you will physically stand out amongst other men who will, in all likelihood, be unaware of their poor body language and standing all in a long row, holding their bottles of beer up to their chests and shifting their eyes nervously toward any attractive woman who walks by.

The fact that you have taken control of what 'state' you are in, gaining a sense of confidence and strength that can come in a moment, will also make a massive difference to how much impact you make when meeting others. By fulfilling the first requirement – taking control – you will already be steps ahead, not only in terms of your appearance and your body language but also in that you now know what to say to a woman and how to say it – how to make verbal impact.

Verbal impact is very important. Let's imagine the girl you have spotted is with her friends, and they are enjoying each other's company when you decide to approach her. Inevitably, she will probably have been approached a few times that night already, so what you say in those first few moments needs to make enough impact to create a shift in her perception and divert her attention. This has to be done to such a degree that she makes the decision to ignore her friends and talk to you instead.

In this situation, it is important to realise that when a group of girls go out together it's very different to a group of guys. For instance, if you were with your friends and a girl spoke to you in a club, your friends would most probably encourage you to talk to her and give you your space. Women, on the other hand, often consider it almost disloyal to temporarily ditch their friends for a man. As a result, the girl's friends will probably try to get her away from you. With that in mind, it goes without saying that if you're making no impact with this particular girl then she will probably see your attempt to interact with her as pointless and go back to her friends.

Nevertheless, irrespective of circumstance, impact can be created the moment you approach a woman. Since you are now in control of your state before actually approaching her, your energy levels will be stronger than that of a man who lacks the control to get into that same desired state. Of course, the opener you use and the way you deliver it will also create more impact than a feeble, "Hey, how are you doing?" or, "Having a nice time?", or a boring, "What's your name?" or "Who are you here with?" You will have the option of introducing yourself in a more unique way. Combined with your recently perfected vocal tone, you will be able to set yourself apart from the rest of the men and create impact!

Impact can be made through the following:

- Your energy or state of mind.
- Your image, style and dress sense.
- Your general conversational skills.
- Your choice of words, questions and answers.
- How you react to her responses and respond to her reactions.
- Your body language (remembering each of the six points/columns of your stage).

Making impact will help you fulfil the next requirement: connection.

CONNECTION

The man who makes chemistry understands that, in order to make a deeper and longer lasting connection, he has to get out of his comfort zone, take a risk and make impact.

Connection can be made with a woman on two levels. The first level is known as the *exterior or surface connection,* which means a superficial level such as finding common interests, opinions you both share and events you might both have experienced. During the early stages of an interaction, this is what you might want to focus on in order to help the conversation flow and to build comfort; it can make people feel comfortable to know they have something in common with a total stranger.

In a world of billions of people, we always feel that the most flimsy connection – such as coming from the same town or sharing the same hobby – is perhaps more important than it actually is. I should stress that finding common interests might be helpful during those early stages but, despite this, they do not guarantee attraction; the lesson detailed in the second step of this book concerning a woman's superficial and ever-changing desires still stands. Nevertheless, exterior connections can help to make you both feel more at ease with each other and also help to build rapport. However, despite this, men often confuse having common interests with a woman as a sure-fire way of getting her to agree to a date. Of course, although connecting on an exterior level will increase your chances, it is never foolproof – and it's always best to try to connect with her on a deeper level.

Let me introduce you to 'by-product'.

When women talk about what they do for a living or what their interests are, it should always be seen as a by-product. Whatever she does or whatever her hobbies are, it is always the result of something deeper, of life experiences or, most importantly, who she is as a person. If you can connect with her at *this* level, then you would have made a connection which is much more long-lasting and therefore more powerful.

For instance, imagine you are talking to a girl and ask her what her job is; she tells you that she is a lawyer. In this situation, you are presented with two choices: you can choose to discuss the by-product which, in this case, is the actual professional role of a lawyer, or you can choose the second option, which is to take the fact that she is a lawyer and use it as a hook point to get to know who she actually is.

Imagine firstly that you decide to take the first option, to carry on partaking in a superficial conversation, which you can then follow up with questions about her job – such as what type of law she practises, how long she has been a lawyer or what law firm she is with. In this instance, although you are learning key information abut this woman's job, the result of these questions will still only keep the conversation on a chit-chat level with no special qualities about it; she's bound to answer these exact same questions with the exact same answers with many different people on a regular basis. There's a high chance she's going to give standard responses to your questions, which will not help at all to make deeper connections!

However, now imagine you decide to take the second option, whereby you want to lead the conversation away from superficial chit-chat and make a deeper connection with her. In this situation, you should start by fulfilling the second element (making a little impact) and say something in response that she wouldn't get asked as often; this will lead the conversation away from the by-product/her exterior interests/job, and instead focus more on her/her feelings and emotions.

The question that follows would be better if it were something like, "Is that something you chose to do, or something your parents wanted you to do?" Now I'm aware that you might initially think that you shouldn't ask her that, but I've seen the results with my students who posed this exact question to women in similar professions, and the response from the women has always been positive; most of them actually welcomed this as a refreshing change from the same old barrage of questions. Unlike the first option, it's thoughtful enough to show the man is interested in getting to know *her* rather than her job. It immediately sets him apart from other men and shows he's making an effort, which also demonstrates his confidence due to the fact that he's unafraid of making an impact.

Of course, there are always exceptions. When practising with my students a few girls seemed slightly puzzled for a moment, but when they saw the guy was not antagonistic but genuinely interested they responded to his question more thoughtfully. Whatever the answer was, it seemed to reveal a lot more about themselves than they usually would so early on in an interaction with a stranger.

Asking what someone does for a living might not be the most original approach, but it does work as a good hook point for taking the conversation to a deeper level. Someone's job says a fair amount about who they are, but how they feel about their job and why they decided to do it reveals a lot more.

To help you use this hook point as a way to connect with a woman on a deeper level, here are a few questions that you should *avoid* responding with when asking what she does for a living. They make little impact and therefore little or no connection will be made:

- Do you like it?
- How long have you been doing it for?
- How did you get into it?
- Where are you based/who do you work for?

Responding with any of these is just lazy and completely uninspiring. Here are some that will make more impact and, as a result, help to make a connection:

- Is that a job you wanted to do since you were little?
- Would you say your job makes you happy – I mean *really* happy and fulfilled?
- I'd never have thought that would be your job. I was thinking you might do something more creative/artistic/ practical/active/work with kids.
- What would you say are the three things that someone needs in order to be good at your job?
- Can you picture yourself doing that same job in ten years? If not, how might it change?
- Is that something you chose to do? Did parents/social pressures play a role? Or did you just fall into it?

If you use a response to her answer like the ones above, you will actually be creating a hairline shift in her perception of you. The moment you ask her what she does (a question we have all been asked a thousand times), she will temporarily put you into the same category as all those other men who asked the exact same question before and will respond with a completely boring follow-up. But the moment you follow up with a more interesting response that makes an impact, and the hairline shift in her perception of you begins. No longer will you be perceived as just another guy with a bunch of boring questions.

This is a prime example of how asking a question which would normally be out of your comfort zone can create impact and, in turn, begin the pattern that ultimately creates a deeper conversation and a more sincere and solid connection.

We will be discussing this throughout the rest of the book; as you develop your conversation skills (with the Nine-Hook Lead System) you will learn how to manipulate the conversation in order to get the woman to reveal more about herself much earlier than she normally would. This will ultimately result in your being able to take the conversation onto a deeper level, thereby making it easier for you to make a significant connection.

There was a man I met a few years ago called Dean. He approached me in a bar in central London. We began chatting. The conversation was fairly light and, if I'm totally honest, all very forgettable. However, after about half an hour, I'd begun to divulge personal thoughts and experiences that I'd usually only share with people I know very well and who I've established trust with. Two hours later I'd forgotten where I was, as I sat in a corner having what could only be described as an amazingly open conversation. I was completely transfixed and, as a result, oblivious to the fact that two hours had passed while my friends were waiting for me to go to the bar we'd planned earlier to visit!

When I eventually realised I had to prise myself away, Dean handed me his number and said (in his Miami Beach twang) that we should continue our conversation another time. Of course, I agreed instantly and gave him my number too.

Three days later, I caught myself thinking about him, checking my phone a few times too many. On the surface, he wasn't really my type and we actually didn't have that much in common. He wasn't interested in politics, while I am, nor the theatre or music; even worse, he was serious about healthy living and keeping fit, topics that sends me straight to sleep. But, despite all that, we'd connected on so many levels; even though our passion was for different things in the exterior sense, we connected via the fact that we actually were passionate people. More importantly, he made me feel like I could really open up to him. He felt like a 'real' person who was genuinely worth getting to know, and demonstrated to me that I was worth getting to know too.

We ended up seeing each other for a few months, but were eventually forced to stop due to the fact he was away too much, going back and forth from his home in Miami. However, I got in contact with Dean again recently. (Thankfully, he was in London, not in a gym somewhere in Florida!) We arranged to meet up at the bar where we had our first encounter two years before.

I told him about how I'd become a female trainer for one of the world's largest pickup companies which, of course, he found very interesting. After the initial banter, I finally came clean and admitted my real reason for wanting to meet up with him again. "I want to pick your brains," I said. I told him I wanted to find out what technique he used to get women to open up so much and connect with them on such a deep level, just like he'd done with me.

"Technique?" he replied, looking genuinely surprised. He looked away and thought for a moment; initially, he seemed unaware that he possessed this great talent. But, as he looked back at me with a cheeky grin, I realised then that I was about to receive a breakdown of the technique that a 'natural' uses.

Dean really is a master of building a deep connection with women – so be sure to take note!

"I picture everyone with a mask," he began. "Their particular mask is something they have chosen for a reason. They wish to be perceived that evening, or day or week, or even their whole life, as the mask they are wearing instead of who they really are. It used to bother me, but then I began to find it fascinating. I love to see the mask slowly slip away." He smiled proudly.

"That's all very poetic, but what my students and I want to know is how you get that mask to slip away," I interrupted.

"This is what I'm teaching," he replied. "The first rule, for lack *of a better term, is to accept that they* are *wearing a mask. If you take everyone at face value and you're naïve enough to think that they're going to display their true selves so early on with a complete stranger, then you make the first error and end up talking about bullshit for the rest of the evening, never attempting to challenge anything they say.*

"The second thing I know is that women love to talk." He stopped to smile at me; when we were dating, he used to say I was a chatterbox. "And they love talking about deeper things and are less afraid to show their emotions than men."

"You mean they let their mask slip quicker than men?" I asked.

"On the whole, yes. Men reserve their deeper emotions for people they really are close to and, as a result of this, their bravado is stronger, they have more to prove. Woman love to get into a gritty conversation and they actually feel relieved when the mask drops."

"That's very true. So, what's the technique?" I pressed on.

"Asking the right questions, not wasting time on irrelevant questions, challenging them in a sincere but never confrontational manner. And when you see the moment they might feel slightly vulnerable, that's the moment you reveal something about yourself, something deep that might surprise them; that's when they realise that you're both sharing a moment and that you're both on the same level; that's the moment you connect as two human beings, rather than just as man and woman."

"You reveal something personal to them and use it as a reward, almost?"

"Yep, like a reward. They tell you something personal, you give them something personal back, so it's not too one-way. They learn that if they keep sharing with you, you will keep sharing back," he answered almost proudly.

And then it all suddenly came back to me: I remembered that, on the night we met, I told him something very private about myself. I also remembered how, after revealing this to him, I felt for just a brief moment that I was slightly exposed. I then realised that he must have sensed this, which was why he responded by telling me something personal about himself.

I asked him if what he'd said about himself all those years ago was true. "Maybe, maybe not, but it worked, didn't it?" he responded.

"Bastard!"

You will find that making deeper connections with women can have some outstanding results, including the ability to eliminate flaky numbers (i.e. when she gives her number but does not pick up the phone or resists meeting with you again).

This will be explained in more detail in Step 12 – 'Closing' – when we take a look at number-closing and phone-call games.

I cannot stress enough how important it is to make deep connection with women. If you manage this, then you will not only alter her perception of you – going from 'cool guy', 'funny guy', 'cocky guy' to 'the man she really wants to see again and again' – but you'll also build up a lot of trust very quickly. Think abut it. She usually she only has these deep discussions and makes deep connections with people she's close to, and here she is opening herself up to you very quickly. Imagine the results you can achieve if you manage to get yourself into the same category as her close friends, lovers and people she trusts.

I am aware that most men wear a mask of bravado that they use to protect themselves with. But are you aware that women wear their own masks, or even in some cases have an alter ego? Men feel slightly vulnerable and exposed when people they do not yet trust begin to see past their mask, but women have a response much closer to a great sense of relief. They feel relieved that they can stop playing the 'mega bitch', or the 'Alpha businesswoman', or the 'sex kitten', or the 'bimbo', or whatever role she's performing for that evening/week/month/lifetime. Remember this, and always accept that what she shows you – or the persona she has decided to display – is very often not the person she really is.

Throughout the rest of this book, we will be referring back to control, impact and connection. Soon you will understand how everything you need to get the best possible results stems from at least one of these three elements.

• STEP SIX •
PRE-APPROACH

The master seducer understands that the interaction starts before a word has been spoken or the eyes have even met.

THE PRE-APPROACH consists of the few moments you have before the interaction begins. And boy oh boy, aren't those few seconds important! In this section we will be looking at how you can get yourself in the appropriate state before talking to a woman, and how to prepare yourself in terms of logistics.

You will also learn how to assess the situation in a discreet fashion; how to extinguish any niggling doubts and last-moment nerves that even the best pickup artists get from time to time; and, most importantly, you will learn the art of never becoming 'outcome-dependent' ever again.

ASSESSING THE SITUATION

Women are masters of this art! We are constantly watching everything. When we go out to a club, we know who is coming through the door and who is leaving; when we see a guy we like the look of, we understand just by observation whether he's popular, whether he has a girlfriend or whether he's gay – and we know all of this very early on!

We posses the skill of assessing the situation and we have it down to a fine art – and this applies to assessing other woman too. We are aware when a stunning woman has walked into the room, and we are also aware if other people are aware of her presence too; we know whether her bag is by a designer or whether it's a fake, and whether her hair colour is from a bottle or whether it's natural. And all of this we manage to do *discreetly*!

But in stark contrast, unfortunately, when men are trying to assess the situation, they usually seem to be oblivious to how obvious they can be! It's almost as if they're in their own bubble and they seem to think it acts as a barrier, whereby no one can see their behaviour – such as when their facial expressions change every time a hot girl walks by, or when they're standing still, staring at a large group of girls, while everyone around them is dancing and having a good time.

So now you're going to get some advice from a woman who, like most other women out there, manages to assess situations without anybody realising it – even though I'm half blind. (I refuse to wear my glasses in public!)

DISCRETION

You might think that you're being discreet and that she hasn't noticed you hovering around her for ages, but be warned! Women are very aware of those guys who hang around for longer than is necessary. When this common scenario takes place, there seem to be two parallel universes in play: on the one hand, the man believes he's being subtle and thinks she's not yet aware of his presence; she, on the other hand, is only too aware! In actual fact, she spotted him from the corner of her eye ages ago, and she knows very well that he's desperately struggling to pluck up the courage to speak to her. Unfortunately, the more he delays the moment, the more he's decreasing his chances by looking like some strange stalker!

When my friends and I go out, we always laugh between ourselves (well, not *me*, obviously, since I'm a little more sympathetic due to the nature of my work) at the guy who aimlessly hovers around us, bobbing his head uncomfortably out of sync with the music. Every time one of us looks over he will nearly always look away, and then back again. He will attempt to smile at us now and again and, more often than not, start looking at an imaginary cell phone text a few times too many.

This whole charade can last for ages. By the time he has clumsily danced his way over to the group from the spot he seemed to have been stuck to, he has unfortunately near-to-zero chance of attracting anyone. And to make matters worse, he is blissfully unaware that he's been the source of our giggling for some time!

Of course, there are plenty of ways you can assess the situation without anyone noticing. For example, if you are going to a bar or a club with a friend, then a great way of checking out the women (and assessing the situation of a *particular* woman), is to have your friend stand in front of you, face to face, while you both talk; never *ever* have him to the side of you, as it will become all too obvious to the woman that you're checking her out.

It's important to note that girls hate going to the bar to get a drink when there is a long line of guys there, all stood shoulder to shoulder. Their heads turn simultaneously as she walks by them and she is fully aware of this – even if those guys think they're being discreet. But if you're talking with your friend face to face, it shows that, unlike the men standing side by side in a long line at the bar, staring at every woman with a pulse, you're there to enjoy the company of your friend(s) regardless of whether there are hot women all over the place. In addition, it shows that you're content to take your time and enjoy your evening at leisure.

The clever part of this is that you can actually get a better idea of the situation around you, without her or her friends suspecting. Now and again you'll look over your friend's shoulder to see what's going on, while he can also be assessing the situation behind you. (In case something better comes along!) By analysing the situation in this way, the two of you literally have eyes in the back of your heads, achieving a 360-degree view of the room.

It's worth noting that women use plenty of subtle signals that we give each other when we spot someone we like, or someone we want to get away from, and it really helps us to communicate (even from a distance). With this in mind, why shouldn't guys create some subtle signals to use themselves?

I think it's funny when, if I'm walking behind two guys in the street, one turns around and spots me and then whispers something to his friend, who will automatically also look behind at me. They think I haven't noticed this, so they carry on walking. And then, suddenly, they'll slow down until eventually they stop dead in their tracks. They then walk over to the nearest shop window and pretend they're interested in something particular, using it as a good excuse to wait patiently for me to go by, just so they can check out the back of me (in case I've got a tail, or something like that). They can't *seriously* think that women don't notice when they do this? But yes, this is a classic example of men thinking they're being discreet when they couldn't be more obvious!

One guy who did this didn't realise what type of shop he'd chosen to pretend to look into. Much to my amusement, I noticed it sold Zimmer frames, walking sticks and thermal pyjamas! As I went past, I told him, "The next time you want to check me out from the back, it's a good idea to pick a shop that doesn't specialise in equipment for the elderly!"

The look on his face was priceless.

So, remember: discretion is the key when assessing the situation.

WHAT YOU ARE LOOKING FOR

A true pickup artist sees less between him and his target compared to most other men. What the average man may see as an obstacle – such as the chance she may have a boyfriend, the possibility of her being a bitch, whether she's with a large group of people (particularly a mixed group) or whether she looks angry or not – a pickup artist or a natural will not be deterred; in fact, his viewpoint will take a 180-degree turn and he will turn some of these so-called obstacles into 'positives'. Here are two examples of how:

- If she looks like a bitch, then maybe everyone else is thinking the same thing; therefore she's probably getting hassled much less than the average friendly-looking girl.
- If she's with a large group of friends, he will see this as a way of making it easier to approach her, as she will feel less vulnerable than if she was on her own or with just one friend. And if she is not attracted to him, then she's always got another few good-looking girlfriends he can get an intro to. (Note: the very fact that a man shows he's not scared of opening a large group of women gives him extra points before he's even finished his first sentence!)

When you have gone out and practised and perfected the techniques in this book, you will perceive fewer obstacles and begin to see every woman as a potential possibility. However, with that said, if you're a beginner, then it's best to not plunge in at the deep end; you don't want to start off approaching mega-bitches or girls who are in long-term relationships, especially since we haven't covered those areas yet. Keep it relatively simple when you start.

As a beginner, you should be considering the following:

- Is she getting hassled a lot? If so, then try to see what the guys seem to be doing that results in their rejection. Watch *how* she rejects them too. Is she being polite or is she being horrible to them? (Again, you must do this discreetly.)
- See who she is with. Is it a mixed group? If so, could one of those guys be her boyfriend?
- If she is in a big group of girls, check to see if she is the Alpha (leader) of the group. If she's not, who is?
- Work out what state she is in. Is she in a high-energy state – dancing, laughing, possibly drinking – and basically showing everyone how much fun she is having? Or is she in a low-energy state – sitting, not laughing much and barely dancing? Assessing her state will allow you to determine what energy state you should approach her with.
- Check out her surrounding area. Work out where you're going to stand or sit if you decide to talk to her. You want to be in the best position possible, so, if she's sitting down, see if there's a nearby chair you can grab or if there's room next to her. You don't want to be crouching next to her knees on the floor for half an hour, and you don't want to be looking down at her for too long either.

OUTCOME DEPENDENCE

The 'she might reject me' excuse is, understandably, the most common reason for a man not to approach a woman. Of course, no one enjoys being rejected, and if you're going into an interaction where you believe there is a high chance of this happening, then it's practically game-over from the start. But you would never go to a job interview thinking you have no chance of getting it, and if you're successful in any competitive sport then you wouldn't compete in a match or tournament with the mindset that you're going to lose. Yet despite this, some may still go into an interaction with an attractive woman that way. So let's change that right now!

There's a problem if, every time you spot an attractive woman, you instantaneously decide that you want to either sleep with her, go on a date with her or, at the very least, get her number. That decision has been made purely based on the way she looks. At this stage, you haven't even entertained the notion that, once you speak to her, you might decide that you're not interested in seeing her – in effect, that *you* might be the one doing the rejecting! As a result you have made yourself completely outcome-dependent. Here follows a technique that I've given my students to counter this.

MARKS OUT OF TEN

First of all, I want you to think of the hottest, sexiest woman that ever lived; the one who is, in your opinion, ten out of ten aesthetically. She could be a famous singer, a model, an actress or, if you're lucky enough, someone you know. Got her in your mind? Good. We will come back to this particular woman in a moment. (My students always seem to say Jennifer Aniston, Scarlett Johansen or Angelina Jolie.)

The next time you spot a hot-looking woman, rather than saying to yourself, "Wow, she's beautiful," or, "She's stunning," or whatever terminology you usually use, I want you to instead start training your mind to have a completely different reaction. I want you to replace the initial thought with a mark out of ten.

Let's say you've spotted a particularly good-looking woman and, in a moment of weakness, given her a nine out of ten. The next thing you must do is stop and then compare her with that hot celebrity woman (or whoever she might be) that I asked you to think of just a moment ago, then ask yourself this: "Is the woman in front of me really only a notch below the most stunning woman ever?" The answer is probably no. How often do you see women looking *that* incredible? Once, maybe twice a year? A nine is an extremely high score, and this mark is given out far too frequently. As a result, it makes the woman seem far more inaccessible than she actually is.

The next stage is to accept the fact that, in comparison to the ten-out-of-ten woman you have in your head, the mark you'll decide to give the woman in front of you will be considerably lower and thus more accurate. This is purely based on visual aesthetics, and so, during this stage, you should also take the time to be fussy: look at her nails, her hair, her makeup, her clothes. Come up with ideas in your mind that you think she could benefit from and which could make her more appealing. Get used to thinking such thoughts as:

- She's nice looking, but if she wore less makeup/more elegant clothes she'd be better.
- She's hot, but her posture is bad. If she sat up straight, rather than slouched, she'd look better.
- If she wasn't chewing gum she'd look more sophisticated.
- She's hot, but those weird facial expressions she keeps pulling make her less attractive.

After spending a few moments being fussy, I want you to then give her the real mark out of ten – which you might now find to be considerably lower. Completing this first part of the technique will help you get the situation into perspective; you will learn to train your mind to have a different reaction to a beautiful woman, and this in turn will calm your nerves and put you automatically in a higher position than her.

CREATING YOUR LIST

This brings me to the second part of the technique.

I often ask my students what they look for in their ideal woman, besides looks. Usually, they give me a fairly vague, unconsidered list of about three or four different aspects. However, it'd be far better if they were to have a more detailed list of what they like and what they *do not* like in a woman, which can ultimately stop them being outcome-dependent.

Why? Because unlike other men who have a vague idea about what they like and dislike in a woman's character, the man who has a clear idea of what he's looking for in a woman will automatically place himself in a higher position before the interaction has even begun! Women have these lists, so why don't you?

Go and write a list right now of what you want and what you don't want in your ideal woman, and divide it into three clear sections as follows:

- Assets – points you feel a woman has to posses in order for you to consider asking her out.
- Bad points – anything that has the potential to put you off of her. (If she has plenty of assets to compensate for the bad points, you should then be willing to overlook some of the latter.)
- Fatal flaws – unacceptably bad points in her character that could seriously jeopardise any chance she has of being asked out on a date by you.

Remember, your list is personal to you and should not be dictated by anyone else. Do not add points simply because you think you *should*. For example, if you like bitchy women (which some men do), then put it into the asset list. Be clear of what you want and do not want, but also acknowledge the fact that, with time, your list will change. You'll find that, as you become more successful, you'll automatically have the luxury of being pickier about your requirements.

THE NEW PRE-APPROACH FRAME OF MIND

When you put these techniques into motion, you should quickly see a noticeable change in your attitude; you will be replacing your old, negative thought processes –"She's so beautiful, I know she'll reject me"; "I know I'm not good enough for her"; "I'm not good enough to approach a girl like that" – with something more positive, more like the following:

"She's cute, pity she's not dressed a little more elegantly. I'm going to have a conversation with her to see what else she has to offer – apart from being cute, that is. If she doesn't meet my requirements, then at the very least I can get an introduction to a friend who might be more suitable."

These new thought processes will stop you from talking to a woman with the sole intention of getting her number or securing a date with her. Instead, after speaking with her, if she meets your requirements then you might consider asking for her number or escalating the interaction. But, until that moment arrives, *you are only approaching her to have a conversation.*

If outcome dependency is holding you back, then apply these techniques to your game and see for yourself how much you benefit from it!

THE OPENER

The successful seducer relies on the quality of his response to her reaction, rather than on the quality of the opening line.

MY STUDENTS OFTEN come to me asking for 'openers that actually work'. They often ask me what the ultimate opening line is, the one that never fails and always produces amazing results. It's almost as if they are on a long quest for the Holy Grail.

If things were that simple and boiled down to just one opening line, I'd be out of a job and men all over the world would be sleeping with a different woman every night of the week! But, in reality – and I'm sorry to break it to you guys – there is no magic opener; there isn't even one that I consider to be a brilliant opener. I know it probably comes as a bit of a letdown for some of you but, as with anything major in life, there is no quick fix!

With this in mind, don't trust anyone who says they have a brilliant opener that will get you laid; if it seems like a good opener then by all means use it – but do not rely on it getting you any results without doing the rest of the work! To illustrate my point further, I want to share with you some openers that my friends and I have had used on us in the past, and leave you to guess which one of these can lead to success:

• You will be my wife someday.

- Hello pretty, are you Italian?
- Excuse me, I have to say that you have the nicest arse I've ever seen.
- Where did you get that tan from?
- I saw you from across the room and wondered if you'd like to join me for dinner?
- Could you be my personal shopper for half an hour?
- Hey! Saw you sitting there looking depressed, and wondered if you want to come to a party me and my friends are going to?
- If I could rearrange the alphabet I'd move the 'I' next to 'U'. [Bursts out laughing at what he's just said.]
- Hello Cinderella, looking for a fella?
- Just wondered if you might want to grab a coffee?

How many of these do you think worked?

The answer is all of them. Yes, even the Cinderella one! It proves that what you decide to use as an opener can range from the ordinarily mundane to the comical cliché. But it is not so much *what* you say as how you say it – to coin another cliché – and, most importantly, its success is reliant on how you follow it up from there.

In order to be successful with the above phrases, all of these men had to set their approach on a strong stage. Their body language would have been solid, the lines executed with perfect vocal tone and, most importantly, the transition from the opener to her response and back would have been smooth.

The guy who came up to me and used the "Hello pretty, are you Italian?" line was responded to with a fairly abrupt, "Uh, no, I'm not." Imagine then if his response to that had been, "Oh . . . uh, okay . . . drink?" If that had been the case, the interaction would have ended there and then and he would have been forgotten about – along with all the other guys who were unable to respond appropriately. But instead, this guy cheekily replied, "What a shame, I'm looking for an Italian girlfriend" – which of course made me curious and forced me to ask why. This then led into a full-blown conversation – and yes, he did end up a happy man.

Take another of the above examples, when the guy told my friend Christine that he wanted to rearrange the alphabet. He delivered the line with this really serious face, slowing down the pace to make it feel as if he wanted to seduce her right there and then. And then, as soon as he finished his terrible cliché and before she had a chance to respond (with what would have been probably a stern, "Fuck off!"), he burst out laughing! There was a pause, and then she realised he was playing with her and so laughed back in turn. He then went on to tell her that he wanted to see what her reaction would be to such a cringe-worthy line. They subsequently ended up dating for eight months.

Unfortunately, however, it ended when he was caught reusing his technique on a girl in a club – although this time the cliché was, "Do you believe in love at first sight or should I walk past again?" And then, right on cue, he burst out laughing – although the laughter stopped when he turned around and saw one of Christine's friends behind him.

Nevertheless, irrespective of which line is used, it's still all about the stage.

Delivery of the opener, and where you take it in relation to her response, is all that matters. Some advanced pickup artists or naturals can even successfully open a woman up non-verbally, simply by using eye contact. Although it's very rare, there have been cases where the man's presence is so sexually powerful that, as a result, he possesses the ability to escalate straight to the kiss without saying even a single word. It can be done but, like I said, this is very rare; irrespectively, however, it proves that the stage plays the most important role in your opener. So remember the six columns that hold up your stage, and be sure not to allow the pressure of the moment to diminish their strength.

Note: I often get my students to practice on me and/or a wing girl in a role-play session, whereby I get them to approach us with the worst opening lines imaginable. Eventually, with a lot of practice, they find they can make the transition to full-blown comfort/conversation with even the most dreadful lines. It's a great exercise to show them how unimportant that opening line actually is.

A MESSAGE ABOUT CANNED MATERIAL

I said before I wrote this book that I wasn't going to waste hard-written pages on canned material when there's so much of it which can be easily found online. You need only type in 'good chat-up lines' or 'canned openers' into a search engine, and voila – you'll be faced with endless website pages. Visit one of these many pages and pick one that you think suits you – I can guarantee you won't be short of choice!

However, I will occasionally give a handful of canned material to my beginner students if they're experiencing a lot of approach-related anxiety, or if they refuse point-blank to go and talk to a woman without a rehearsed or canned opener. In this situation, the openers I choose for my students will nearly always be opinion openers that usually start with, "Hey, can I get a quick female opinion on something?" These include getting an opinion on:

- What type of tattoo he should get.
- What present he should buy for his friend (who happens to be a girl).

- What he should do in a certain situation/dilemma that he's in.
- What costume he should wear for a fancy dress party he's been invited to.
- What type of theme he should have for a party he wants to organise.

I favour these particular openers because each one will guarantee that the girl will respond with a 'high-calibre hook' (something we'll be covering in the next step, relating to conversation skills).

If you want to use canned openers then by all means do so, but be aware that what you generate from her as a response to your opener is the important part, and you must ultimately use her chosen response/hook point to make the transition away from your original opener, both smoothly and quickly.

Since the pickup community has grown in the last few years, thanks to media exposure many women have become much more aware that there are men out there who are using pickup lines to seduce them. Obviously, if a woman has even a slight suspicion that you're using a line on her, she will become immediately defensive. Chances are you will fail to even get into a conversation with her, let alone sleep with her.

Fairly recently, I went out to a bar and overheard two girls in the toilets discussing the fact that two separate men – who, coincidently, didn't know one another – had come up to them and used a line which is very well known in the community: "Excuse me, can I get your opinion on something? Who lies more, men or women?"

I've also experienced something similar to this, whereby I was sitting on the train, just minding my own business, when a man sat down next to me and began a long story about how his friend was getting married to a girl he believed was untrustworthy; he was undecided as to whether he should tell his friend or stay quiet, and said he needed my honest female opinion.

This is called the 'my best friend' opener, and is very well known. I smiled politely at the man, and handed him my business card. He called a few days later and booked a session with me.

Be aware that this community is growing FAST; so, as time goes by, I want you to create your own material and keep on changing your openers.

• STEP EIGHT •
CONVERSATION SKILLS AND THE NINE-HOOK LEAD SYSTEM

The man who makes chemistry must master the art of conversation, in order to maximise his personality to the best of his ability.

STUDENTS COME TO me with a variety of sticking points; the common problems are usually approach-related anxiety, keeping clear of the 'let's just be friends' zone, understanding what women want, body language and learning how to effectively escalate the interaction into a more sexual encounter. But by far the most common problem my students have are these conversational ones:

- Running out of things to say.
- The inability to make the transition from opener to full-blown conversation (the comfort stage).
- Dead ends in conversation.
- Uncomfortable silences.
- Interrogation-style questioning.
- Conducting a boring, dull or uninspiring conversation.

Let's take a scene from one of those well-scripted American sitcoms like *Friends*. One of the guys approaches a beautiful woman in that coffee shop they seem to be in all the time. The girl nearly always responds to his opener with a pleasant and positive response and the conversation always seems so effortlessly smooth; she laughs at his jokes, she responds by asking him questions about himself and, after some wonderfully witty lines, she agrees to go on a date with him that very evening. Thanks to a team of talented scriptwriters, the entire scenario looks easy and unproblematic. But, in the harsh light of reality, when you go out and try to replicate that great scene you realise that, without the writers and without that lovely responsive girl, your ability to make the conversation lead to her acceptance of a date is near impossible.

Wrong!

It can be done. At first, it will be with a tremendous amount of effort and concentration on your part, but, with the system you are about to learn – backed up of course by as much practice as you can possibly manage – you will soon be able to avoid those uncomfortable silences, dead ends and boring conversations which ultimately lead nowhere, and instead become a master conversationalist – even with the most difficult and unresponsive of women!

Remember that being a master of conversation is not enough on its own to attract women. But, if you can master the six points of the stage plus this technique, then the results could give you more power than you realise.

"BUT I CAN TALK SO WELL WITH MY FRIENDS"

A lot of my students are very frustrated about this because when they are with their friends/colleagues/families, etc, they are able to have great conversations. They come across as funny, witty, challenging and interesting. Yet, when they talk to a woman they are attracted to, they often find that all the conversational skills they possess go out of the window!

There are two reasons for this: the first is because of time constraints. If you are talking to a woman who is sitting down at a bar, then you have perhaps about ten minutes before she decides whether she wants to carry on talking to you or not. If you're her physical type then you might get an extra five or ten minutes, which leaves around 20 minutes for you to hook her in. Yet if you are talking to her in the day, then often the time constraints will be tighter. For instance, say she's waiting for a bus; in that particular situation you probably only have around five minutes. If she's walking in the street and is in a rush to get somewhere, you have at best about 30 seconds! Time constraints will undoubtedly put anybody under a considerable amount of pressure and, as we all know, when we are under pressure we panic, and when we panic our mind can go blank!

The second reason why men suddenly find that all their conversational skills disappear is because of the outcome-dependency issue, increasing the amount of pressure the guy feels in an interaction with a hot woman. Within time, by following the advice I've given in the pre-approach chapter, you will become less and less outcome-dependent.

THE NINE-HOOK LEAD SYSTEM

Let me introduce to you the original Nine-Hook Lead System, which I've been teaching my students. It comes as no surprise to me that most of my students have heard of this technique through word of mouth, and immediately ask me to teach it to them before anything else. Understandably, they're eager to learn how to take the opener to a full-blown conversation within a couple of minutes, but I always tell them – as I'm telling you now – that everything you've learned from the book so far must first be perfected before trying to implement this system.

It's important to realise that being a master conversationalist will not guarantee your success with women; it's a skill you will learn, and the knowledge that you gain from it will, in itself, empower you and diminish the fear you previously had of not knowing what to say, or running out of material too early on in the interaction, thus helping to destroy approach anxiety.

HOOKS

I'm about to give you some powerful insights to the female mind, so use this information wisely.

From now on I want you to see every word she says as a hook, which is an important first point. Whatever comes out of her mouth offers you one of nine available paths; which path you decide to take depends on you, the situation and the woman's attitude, but the range of options that her hook gives to you is very empowering in it self.

HIGH-CALIBRE AND LOW-CALIBRE HOOKS

You must remember, however, that there are both useless and useful hooks.

Low-calibre hooks are the words she gives you which are difficult to respond to, including one-word answers such as 'no', 'yes' and 'fine'. You do not want to generate these kinds of useless hooks from her during the early stages, yet men all over the world are doing exactly that! For example, some men go up to a girl in a bar, and initiate the following conversation:

"You enjoying yourself?"
She responds with, "Yes."
He then asks, "How are you?"
She responds with, "Fine."

He then proceeds to ask her if she comes here often.
She answers, "No."

And there you have it – a classic example of a man who has generated only low-calibre hooks and, because of this, has made it difficult for the two of them to move into a conversation from the opening.

By the time the man has something interesting to say or has made a connection, she has usually already decided that the interaction is pointless and will find her excuse to move away. At this point, he's totally unaware that he's generating useless hooks and, in doing so, making it increasingly difficult to move the opener/introduction stage to the comfort stage.

As I mentioned in the last chapter, one of the reasons that I occasionally give canned openers to my students is simply so that they are able to generate a high-calibre hook almost instantly, making the conversation easier to develop. For instance, say you take the opener, "My friend's gone away, and I need to buy his girlfriend a present," you'd then be aiming for a higher calibre hook instead of a low one. Even if you ask the girl where she got her tan, you would still be aiming for a high-calibre hook.

Below is a diagram that I give to my students as a quick reference point, in order for them to understand how the calibre system works. At the high end of the scale are the hooks you should be aiming for in order to make it easier for yourself; as you go further down the scale, you'll reach the hooks you should avoid generating for the woman in the early stages of the interaction.

At the top end of the scale, we have various hooks, including jobs, interests, hobbies, countries (of nationality or residence), favourite genres, celebrities, books and films; all of these are great when using the Nine-Hook Lead System. For example, one

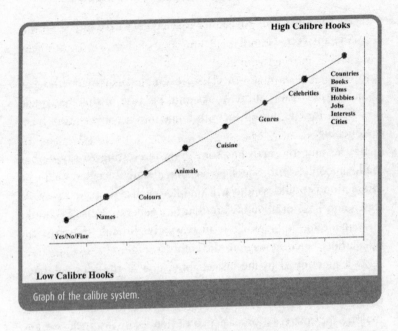

Graph of the calibre system.

common question that guys asks girls with a foreign accent is where they are from, their country of origin providing an extremely high-calibre hook. If you asked a girl what film she would recommend you to watch, again you would be generating a high-calibre hook, likewise if you asked a girl what her hobby or perhaps her job is.

I hear you querying whether the calibre of hook depends on her answer rather than the category – i.e. what country she's from, what actual job she has, or whether you know the film or book she recommends to you – but the answer to this is that, although it's an added bonus that you both share the same job or come from the same town, it's not a guarantee that the conversation will flow easily; however, with the Nine-Hook Lead System you will understand that the actual country or book or whatever is irrelevant. It is the calibre level of the hook that matters.

Being dependent on the chance that you'll be familiar with the hook you generate from her is a limiting belief that I want to help you change, starting from now.

Remember this: most of the other men out there hope to have something in common with her; they're all hoping that her response to their question will be something they can relate to, such as her favourite film, or her hobby or job. As a result of all of this hoping for common ground, the man is missing fantastic opportunities to make the transition from the opener/early stages of the interaction to a full-blown conversation.

You need to learn to separate yourself from this thought pattern. Instead of simply hoping, like the other guys out there, start to learn the system. You'll then gain a deep understanding and enough knowledge to be able to effectively respond to whatever information she gives you, regardless of whether you're familiar with the book or the film she's recommended to you, or whether you have even heard of the city she's from. By learning this system, you can respond to every hook she gives you in nine different ways.

(Nine options! How can you ever reach a dead end again?).

The master seducer does not restrict himself to only seeking those who share his interests or who say what he wants them to say.

HOOK LEAD ONE: OPEN QUESTION

This is the first hook lead. There is no particular order for them but I tend to start with this one, as it's the easiest and most commonly used.

An open question can only be responded to with an open answer, meaning that her answer will have to consist of more than one word. Your aim is for her to speak as much as possible during that early stage, to get her into her comfort zone. The more someone speaks, the more comfortable they become; the more comfortable they become, the more they speak.

Here is an example of an open question:

"I'm going on a long flight and was wondering if you could recommend me a good film I can watch on my DVD player?"

She answers, "*Dirty Dancing.*"

At this point your initial reaction is probably that you have already seen it, or you don't like it. But instead of saying this and cutting the conversation off before it's even started, you could respond with an open question, which would be either:

"Why *Dirty Dancing*?" or "What's it about?" or "Why do you like *Dirty Dancing* so much?"

And let's say she responds with, "I love the eighties soundtrack and the story." As you can see, open questions are very easy and they can lead to multiple hooks. For instance, if you don't want to get into a conversation about a film you don't like or don't even know, then the hooks she gives you in response to the open question will come in useful, enabling you to move away from the initial opener.

In this example, her response to your open question provides you with two great new topics of conversation: the 1980s and music. From here you can very quickly move on from the opener, simply by using the hooks she's given you as a response to your open question.

The open question is good to use early on so that you can avoid getting stuck in the 'interrogation' pattern, which involves you asking a closed question and her, in response, giving a closed answer – which you then respond to by asking another closed question, before she gives you another closed answer . . .

This is something which happens all too often – we call it an interview or interrogation-style conversation, and it should be completely avoided!

HOOK LEAD TWO: FACT

A fact should always start with, "Did you know . . . ?" or, "Are you aware . . . ?" and then you can follow on with a fact based on the hook she's given you. This is a great way of taking the pressure off the 'it's just me and you' situation, which can be a little too intense early on in the interaction. You can also introduce another element into the discussion, in this case the little facts you share with her in relation to the hook she's given you. This can move the conversation away from her and thus relieve any pressure she might have been experiencing; as a result, she will welcome discussing the hook point.

In general, people respond fairly well to quirky little facts about things they thought they knew so well. It's a little trick I use when I meet people who might be slightly nervous or shy. When I sense they feel uncomfortable with people who want to get to know them too soon, I find that asking where they're from and responding with a little fact I know about their town or city seems to relax the situation a bit. In return, because they feel it's moved the spotlight off them, they tend to respond well and subsequently open up more.

The 'little fact' can be genuine or possibly something less accurate. If you know an interesting little nugget of information about the country she's from or the job she does, then use it. Unfortunately, not all of us are walking encyclopaedias of useless information, so a lot of my students ask me what they should say if they don't actually know any facts at all about the hook they've been given. My response is that they could make up a 'fact' – and it can work just as well, if not better!

HOOK LEAD THREE: OPINION

Here we move nicely onto the third hook lead, which I like to refer to as one of the 'emotional reaction leads'. Unfortunately, men often avoid opinions in the early stages of the conversation, while the man who uses this hook lead and the other emotional reaction leads is often the most successful, as it shows his lack of fear in expressing himself and demonstrates his decision to not bend his own reality in accordance with hers. It also forces us girls to respond with a question about him, as we become curious as to why he has this opinion.

Your opinion relative to her response should never be too wishy-washy early on in the interaction; you should not use 'neither here nor there' phrases or responses, such as 'that's okay' or 'that's nice', etc. When you respond with a vague opinion about something she might love, or one of her regular activities, you will discourage her from discussing that particular subject further with you. When it comes to stating your opinion, my advice is to get out of your comfort zone, take a small calculated risk and respond to what she's said by either saying you love it or hate it. Don't be afraid to create a little impact, and making impact *does* involve taking a risk.

But obviously, you must always apply commonsense when using the opinion hook lead. In this case, saying you hate something very close to her heart – like her job, her religion or a particular passion she has – is obviously going to be too hurtful and could ultimately come across as insulting. Instead, be sure to restrict the negative opinions to subjects that she can detach herself from, such as her favourite book, favourite film or favourite holiday destination.

When men talk to women and agree with everything they say, holding back their true opinions by simply responding with phrases of agreement, it can make the interaction very boring and subsequently lead to the dreaded 'nice guy' factor. In addition, it can also cut dead a conversation. So often I've had a guy ask me where I've recently been on holiday, and in response – no matter where the country – he says something like, "That sounds nice." Which leads me to decide that I really don't want to discuss my holiday with an unenthusiastic person who doesn't care where I've been at all.

The funny thing in this situation is that I really don't mind if a guy says to me, "Really? You went there? I've never seen the attraction of that place. I don't know why people love it so much." This would be enough to provoke me to explain to him why it was such a great place to visit, and it sets me a little challenge to try and change his mind.

Your opinion might also force the girl to ask you why you hold it. This is a great way to change the pattern of the conversation, because it gets her used to asking you questions rather than always the other way around.

Often, when we meet a guy who voices his own opinion early on in the interaction, we see him as a refreshing change from all the 'head nodders' out there; it gets us curious to find out why he thinks differently and different opinions provoke us to ask questions in turn. I've never once heard a woman say she liked a guy because he shared her opinion on everything – usually it's quite the opposite! However, there should be a sense of balance. If you're disagreeing with everything she says, this will only tire her and bring her state down; nevertheless, apply this approach now and again and do not be afraid to voice your opinions. (Remember: everything in moderation.)

When it comes to voicing your opinions, make sure that – irrespective of her reaction – you do not back down from what you've said. Of course, I'm fully aware that this can lead to a heated debate (and we all know that heated debates can sometimes lead to full-blown arguments!) but have no fear, because I'm going to share with you a great technique that you can use in any situation which might require a degree of argument. This technique has helped my students so much that some of them now go out of their way to have an argument or debate, just so that they can use it.

THE DEFUSION TECHNIQUE

At some point in the debate or argument (preferably before it gets personal), you must take control of the frame and say to her, "Stop"; keep eye contact and smile; pause and then say, "It's obvious we are not going to agree about this. Even if we sit here for two weeks and carry on, we will never agree. Am I right?"

She will probably agree with this logic, so then you say: "But you know what? That's actually good, I like the fact that you're someone like me, who never backs down. Most people just agree with the other person for the sake of it, but you're someone who speaks their mind regardless. I love that in people." You could also say, "It's great to meet a girl who feels so strongly and speaks her mind, most girls just end up agreeing out of politeness." She will be left with no other option but to smile in agreement.

This approach will not only defuse the situation and allow you to both maintain your point of views without either one having to back down (something which hot-headed people hate to do!), it's also a great way for you to show her that, although you differ in an opinion, you still connect on something far greater. By using this technique you're getting her to realise that you both share a similar nature, in that you're both passionate and strong-minded people.

It's important that you should never be afraid of getting into a debate or light argument with a girl. Now that you know the defusion technique, use it wisely and carefully, and understand what it can gain for you.

HOOK LEAD FOUR: CHALLENGE

Here we have the other hook lead that causes an emotional reaction. There are two ways to challenge her: seriously, on an intellectual level (challenging on the subject of politics is something that I've noticed French girls particularly love), which can also sometimes lead to a heated debate (which of course can be defused – see above).

The second way is by challenging her in a more playful manner, which means winding her up or teasing her. But let it be clear that you're only playing with her and mean no harm.

An example of a playful challenge:

Guy: "What do you do for fun?"
Girl: "I love driving my car in the countryside."
Guy: "I bet you're a terrible driver." He smiles.
Girl: "No, I'm a very good driver," she retorts.
Guy (pauses for a moment, and looks back at her quizzically, stroking his chin): "Nah, I reckon you go zooming through red lights and knocking down old ladies."

Because the assumptions are unrealistic and his manner is playful, she will realise that she was a little too hasty to defend herself so seriously. Again, this gives the power of the interaction an extra nudge into his side of the court.

The message I wish to get through to you concerning this particular hook lead is to stop looking at challenges as though they're negative; this is the excuse 'nice guys' use to stop themselves taking any risks, in order to ensure no risky impact is made. But it's important to realise that challenges can have positive results – so use them! (And remember that, no matter how bad an argument might get, there is always the defusion technique.)

HOOK LEAD FIVE: HUMOUR

My friends and I often comment on the fact that our male friends are usually funnier than our girl friends. Yet when we go on a date with a guy, he often seems to lack all sense of humour. We might see him in a different social situation, e.g. with his friends, and then he suddenly comes across as really funny. You may also have noticed that when *you* go out on a date with a girl, or if you're simply just chatting her up, the sense of humour that your friends love about you seems to disappear.

But this is a massive part of your personality! If someone erased my personal sense of humour, I would no longer be who I am. And of course, your own particular humour is another hook lead at your disposal.

There is nothing more personal to you than what makes you laugh. This is something that everyone in the world possesses but, unfortunately, most people don't always know how to use it to their advantage; they don't realise that a person's sense of amusement can be a very powerful tool, instead seemingly preferring to keep it buried away as if they were ashamed of it.

Men hide their sense of humour mainly because they're too worried whether she will find it funny or not (outcome dependency again). But let me give you a tip: if you say something in response to what she said and you consider it amusing, yet it's clearly obvious that she doesn't get it, then what you do next is much more important than the actual joke.

Often, a man will say something he considers to be funny, only to be met with a blank expression, and a negative process begins to take place. First, his smile will begin to look painfully stuck to his face; then his eyes will probably start shifting around the room as he begins to think of a quick change of subject. The uncomfortable silence becomes deafening. Sometimes he'll even clear his throat to disguise the initial laughter, and eventually the woman watching him will either roll her eyes or smile with pity at the poor bag of nerves in front of her – and any passion that might have occurred that evening has been promptly extinguished. (Sound familiar?)

The most effective way of handling a situation like this is to simply look her straight in the eye and acknowledge her lack of enthusiasm. Do it by saying with a cheeky smile, "You didn't find that funny, did you?" At a minimum, this shows her that your witty response was not for her pleasure, but for your own. Whether she laughed or not does not determine how you feel. You could even respond with, "I thought that was really funny myself. Oh well, it's a shame you don't share my sense of humour" – once again holding that unshakeable eye contact. You could even make it more playful (if you're feeling bold enough) and say, "Well, I guess that's it, this will never work!" – ensuring that you do this in a playful manner. (This is, of course, role-play, whereby you're pretending you're already a couple and you've already dumped her.) More often than not, saying something like this can force the girl to giggle.

Ever heard the expression 'the elephant in the living room'? What it means is that the elephant, like your joke, becomes more uncomfortably obvious the more that people try to ignore it (like an annoying twitch that someone might have at a dinner party). In this scenario, the best thing to do is talk about it and bring the fact that she didn't get the joke to the forefront of the conversation.

Another important point is that the man who cracks jokes simply in order to make the girl laugh can very quickly fall into the role of 'court jester'. I've written many articles and online blogs about men who play the jester, which involves him trying to make all the girls laugh and keeping everyone's spirits high, and yet, when it comes to the end of the night, he doesn't actually seem to be sleeping with the women he's kept amused and happy all evening! The reason for this is simple: like the court jester, he becomes a loveable but weak character; like the jester, he is there for the pleasure of others and is easily used to fulfil a short-term need. Consequently, he's often forgotten about quickly; like the court jester, he's dispensable.

People of the medieval court would clap for the jester as he performed for them, and he would ask for nothing in return. Nevertheless, when the banquet commenced, he was not invited to sit at their table and was either ignored or forgotten about. Fast forward into the future and we still now have those same jesters (but without the belled hats!); he's the guy who's always good for a laugh, the token funny guy that people like to small-talk with. Any moment that the conversation takes a slump, he will automatically say something funny and the people he's with will have their spirits refreshed and will feel good, because he has served his purpose. (Most of us know several people like this.)

For the jesters, the focus is on the end result of his audience, but the man who uses his personal sense of humour for his own personal amusement is in a far better position. Unlike the modern-day court jester, he is, in fact, a judge; he likes to test people and have his own fun.

I can hear you saying now as you read this, "But I know guys who make everyone laugh and get the girls!" My response to this is, "I know them too!" In particular, I know one guy called Terry, who I've been friends with now for almost a decade. He is so funny, and I consider him to be one of those few people able to please everyone with his sense of humour; not only that, but he gets a lot of women. I asked him how he remains funny, how he makes nearly everyone he meets laugh, and how he does this without becoming the court jester.

"Because I'm amusing myself," Terry replied.

I was intrigued.

"I have never, and will never, make another person laugh if I myself do not find it funny. Why on earth would I say something to keep another person entertained? I'm not a clown on a stage!"

I asked him how he felt when the occasional person didn't laugh.

"Then they don't get my humour and will remain out in the cold, bewildered. I'm certainly not going to adjust my sense of humour, it's part of who I am."

His arrogance, I felt, was part of his style of humour. Unlike the buffoon, Terry carries an air of authority and it's immaterial to him whether a woman he likes gets it or not; in fact, Terry went on to say that it sometimes amuses him even more when people *don't* get him, which in turn seems to have an interesting effect when they begin to want in on the joke – she may have had a noticeable lack of interest at first, but now she doesn't want to look stupid because she doesn't get it.

Personal amusement is a very positive tool, so if you decide to say something that you think is funny in response to her hook, make sure you're not outcome-dependent in terms of her reaction. Obviously, it's a massive bonus if she shares your sense of humour and laughs with you too but, if she doesn't, then just remember to bring the fact that she doesn't get what you said to the forefront of the conversation. Always do this in a relaxed and cheerful manner, and never in a way that could give the impression that you're angry or upset.

Enjoy your own sense of humour and use it to your advantage.

The successful seducer will not allow her reaction to affect his state.

HOOK LEAD SIX: ANECDOTES

In the area I used to live in with my parents, there was a middle-aged man who I noticed was always in the local pub. Anytime I passed by that pub, I'd look in the window and see him perched on his usual stool at the end of the bar. He'd go in there every day with his scruffy brown dog, who'd contentedly sleep under the stool. Apparently, this man had been going into the pub nearly every day for over 20 years, and I calculated that this meant almost half his life as he couldn't have been over 50.

Anytime I happened to go in there, I noticed that he always seemed to have an audience around him which included men and women of all different ages. I also noticed that he always seemed to be doing all the talking while the audience just listened with interest. Initially I didn't pay much attention, but, being a curious creature at heart, I asked the barman one day why this man always had so many people around him.

"He's been coming here for years, we call him 'the Storyteller'," said the barman.

I looked over at the so-called Storyteller, who seemed to be in the process of describing something with great enthusiasm. I rolled my eyes and turned back to the barman. "Oh I see," I said, rather dismissively. "You mean he's one of those guys who have seen everything and done everything but, in reality, have done fuck-all in their lives and just tell tall stories that never really happened?" (My language can be quite vulgar.)

The barman laughed. "Not at all. He tells very simple stories, you know, just small everyday stuff, but the way he tells them is unique. It's kinda strange but, when you listen to him, you get sucked in and forget about everything else around you."

I became more curious at this stage, and slowly made my way over to the bar and stood near where the Storyteller and his *audience were gathered. As I pretended to examine the lunchtime menu written up behind the bar, I listened to the conversation.*

I immediately noticed that the man had a faint Irish accent, which seemed to get stronger whenever he reached a part of the story where something dramatic was happening. He made wonderful gestures with his hands, his arms and his face, and used his entire body to illustrate the story to his listeners. I also listened to the words he was using; they were very descriptive and seemed to connect the listeners both emotionally and mentally, but what stood out most for me was the fact that his story was very simple.

I realised he was telling the audience about a visit to the vet the day before, because his dog had not been eating properly. It was very mundane. If anyone else had been telling this story, I imagine nobody would have taken the time to listen. But he seemed to captivate the listeners by telling them all about the other pets in the waiting room and their owners too, how the vet had handled the situation and how he reminded the Storyteller of his old schoolteacher – whereby he proceeded to recite a funny little anecdote about how he'd played a particularly cruel trick on this teacher over 30 years ago! The man's audience laughed and, after he'd finished the story, instead of turning their backs to carry on with whatever they'd been doing beforehand, they asked him questions and seemed to want to get to know him more and more – and I was no exception; I was hooked.

Later on, I thought about how this little story was spectacularly told and imagined how, if this man had led a really amazing life (rather than going to a pub every day), his stories would have been legendary. In my mind I compared him with another man I knew who really did lead an exciting life; he was a playboy and had travelled the world, doing everything from sleeping with famous supermodels to spending time in prison. He was full of amazing stories and yet, despite all of these crazy events and a life packed full of interesting occurrences, he was one of the most boring people I'd ever met! He would tell these potentially amazing stories but would leave his listeners uninspired. The content was brilliant but his execution of them was terrible; they were either rushed or long-winded, and his manner was detached from his audience. He was the complete opposite to the Storyteller, who told stories of very simple events but told them artistically, leaving his listeners inspired and captivated.

Storytelling is a fine and beautiful art. A well-developed and well-presented story can cut across age barriers and hold the interest of a vast spectrum of different people, reaching many listeners on many different levels. Good stories – and their tellers – will be remembered long after more formal orations. As such, anecdotes and stories are a great way for you to create multiple hooks and threads, which both you and her can pick up on.

However, as with the other hook leads, there is a correct way of giving an anecdote and a wrong way. When done the wrong way, the anecdote is either so long that the listener is bored or so short that it seems almost pointless to mention. As a result, the listener feels she has next to nothing to respond to. On the other hand, when an anecdote is told correctly it can result in a multitude of possibilities.

The way an anecdote should begin is to take the hook she has handed you and link it with a story, preferably relating to your own life – although it can be something which happened to someone you know. Make sure that it's a fairly short story, as the trick is to make it into an epic – although note that it should never be the other way around, whereby you take a long, complicated story and make it short.

To make your anecdote interesting and achieve effective results, ensure it contains these four factors:

- **Inclusion (adding 'follow-up threads')**
- **Timing**
- **Emotion**
- **Description**

By using each of these four factors, you can maximise your results. 'Inclusion' means including the woman in the story. You can do this by asking – or even assuming – certain things about her in relation to your story while you're telling it. For example, you might be telling the story of when you went to a club and met a celebrity, in which case it's a good idea to pause a few times and ask her whether she's a fan of this particular celebrity, or whether she's been to that particular club before. In conclusion she will at least answer either 'yes' or 'no', which you should acknowledge briefly before continuing with the story (while making a mental note of her response).

Later on, as you get nearer to the end of the story and have added these small inclusions a few times, you'll find that as a result you've created multiple 'follow-up threads', which are absolutely necessary because she'll be able to pick up on at least one of those questions or assumptions you made, which will make the conversation flow smoothly and result in improved rapport. Even if she's one of those really unresponsive girls and does not actively pick up on any of the threads, there is always the option of you picking up on them yourself.

For instance, let's say that you've finished telling the story and, in response, she simply smiles politely but doesn't actively pick up on one of the many follow-up threads you put in the anecdote (although, more often than not, the girl usually will). Instead, rather than thinking of a whole new topic or waiting in awkward silence, you should take the lead by continuing with one of the threads. For example: "So, you say you're a fan of [the celebrity you were taking about]? That's cool. Most people don't like his work. Which of his films do you like best?"

Whether she responds by going back to one of the threads or you do is irrelevant; either way, the outcome will provide a seemingly natural progression from the anecdote onto the other points, which is yet another way of moving the early interaction into a full-blown conversation.

As for the second of the four factors, timing is important in storytelling: it builds dramatic tension and demonstrates your ease at being in the spotlight; someone who rushes his words can make the interaction seem too hasty, which will definitely not help in building comfort. Instead, ensure you pause for effect; speed up certain parts of the story when you wish to create a sense of drama; lower your voice in other parts to build tension.

The third factor is emotion, which needs to be present in your voice. Using emotionally powerful words is a great way to produce emotional reactions; it can change moods and get her into the same state as you when you're telling the story or recalling a particular moment. (Try to steer clear of unemotional words such as 'nice' or 'cool'; they don't really make much impact on the listener.)

Use words which will anchor her emotions, this will force her to 'emotionally invest' in you. One pickup artist I know always manages to get a particularly sad story into the conversation. Some people may feel this is a bad idea, as it might make her feel depressed and lower the energy of the interaction. But remember, us girls enjoy a sad film; we actually get the box of tissues ready and enjoy a good old weep! This is because the sad emotions we feel when watching a sad movie or hearing a sad story occur within a contained situation and are not our own reality. So tell her any type of story you want, but be sure to use words that anchor her emotionally. Getting her to emotionally invest in you is more important than you can imagine.

Lastly, description is the key in making that short story into an epic, thus creating a memorable moment between you and the woman in question. People who are not masters in the art of storytelling tend to rush over the details and descriptions, which is a shame as description is a key to making the story come alive. Instead, nervous storytellers worry about being boring and wasting the listener's time, so they head to the punch-line or the point of the story far too quickly for anyone to actually enjoy the process! Again, this has the unfortunate effect of making the interaction seem rushed.

Remember that, by using description, the listener can gain access to a peephole into your life; instead of seeming one-dimensional when the character disappears at the end of the story, you demonstrate other aspects of your life which can help her get to know you a little more.

Women LOVE detail! Women see each tile in the mosaic whereas men see the big picture that the mosaic displays.

It is extremely important to perfect your anecdotes, and ensure that you get the conversation threads in there too; I cannot stress enough how helpful they will be to you! Remember that you should not avoid anecdotes because you feel your story is boring, or that you believe you've not had an exciting James Bond experience yet. By including the four factors you can make nearly any story interesting, plus you'll be flooding the conversation with fresh new hooks.

HOOK LEAD SEVEN: TASKS

This is one of my favourite hook leads. It involves a task being performed, and can be done without the need of a hook, such as getting her to hold your coat while you go to the bathroom, or to stand up and turn around so you can check out her jeans (her arse). But it can be used in a much more subtle way when applied as a hook lead.

If, for example, the girl says she is from Sweden, the obvious thing to get her to do is to tell you something in Swedish. Although this is essentially a task, it is nevertheless something she will often have been asked to do. (It happens a lot. I have a friend from Portugal who gets asked to say stuff in Portuguese all the time!) Because this question is not original to her, she will not find it entertaining at all, only repetitively boring and unimaginative. But if you were to add something a little different, such as getting her to say something ridiculous or filthy in Swedish, that might be a better idea; it's always advisable to think a little outside the box.

When using the task lead, I prefer my students to use the one that goes, "Tell me three interesting facts about Sweden," or, "I heard it's a great place, tell me three things that makes Sweden so cool." *Where is the task here?* I hear you ask. It's in the 'tell me' part right at the beginning – subtle, but still effective. 'Tell me' and 'show me' are not the same as 'can you please tell me?' or 'please could you show me?', which is more like asking her permission than getting her to perform a task. It's a small play on words, and although she won't consciously be aware that you're getting her to perform a task, she'll know on a subconscious level.

The more you do this, the more likely it will be that she'll accept doing more obvious tasks later on in the interaction; this is because you've got her used to obliging your more subtle tasks, thus the pattern you've started will be easy to continue. Remember this at the end of the interaction when you tell her to put her number in your phone. The pattern of task-setting should continue. (We will discuss this in greater detail in Step 12.)

The other reason why telling her to name three things in relation to the hook is incredibly useful is because it'll automatically give you three new hooks! For example, let's say you know nothing about Sweden and/or have no real desire to carry on with that particular subject. If you were then to give her the task of telling you three great things about it, she'll respond in her sexy Swedish accent: "It's great because there are some beautiful views of the mountains. Um . . . it has a fantastic nightlife where people party hard and . . . hmm, what else? Um . . . I have all my family and friends there who I miss very much. That's why I think Sweden is great!"

Bingo! She has introduced three interesting hook points that you can then continue with. For example:

- "Are you really such a party animal? I had you down for the quiet girl who's in bed by 10:30!"
- "It's difficult to leave your friends and family behind. You must have found that decision really hard to make?"
- "The mountains? Most girls would never mention the scenery in their country, that's cool. You admire natural beauty, so do I."

As you can see, this is a great way to move nice and smoothly away from the original question while simultaneously getting her to perform a task.

HOOK LEAD EIGHT: VALIDATION

Here is not only the most important hook lead but one which centres round the most important things a man can ever learn about building up his levels of attraction. Due to its paramount importance in relation to your game, it's only right that this lead is assigned its own step, and so we will cover it in the next chapter.

HOOK LEAD NINE: ASSUMPTION

Assumptions are a great hook lead to use and are also a good option to replace questions, which are often overused. An assumption is when you respond to her hook point by beginning with either, "I reckon . . ." or, "I would say . . .", which clearly show her you're making an assumption rather than asking a question – again a subtle yet effective play on words.

There are two simple points you need to follow in order to make an effective assumption:

- **Add detail.**
- **Know where to go next if your assumption is wrong.**

By adding detail, you avoid making a vague assumption. The general rule to remember here is that you want to make it seem as if you've tailor-made the assumption just for her, rather than something which could apply to any other girl in the room. For instance, imagine you ask the girl what she likes to do in her spare time, and she replies, "Shopping." Then you reply, "I reckon you shop at the top stores, like Harrods"; it's an okay assumption, but ask yourself whether it's enough for her to respond with anything else other than, "Yes, I do," or, "No, I don't." Loads of girls go to this kind of upmarket shop, so it would have been a better idea to add a little more detail to the assumption. For example: "I reckon you shop at Harrods and all the top stores, but secretly you love to hunt for bargains in second-hand shops, rummaging around, searching for a treasure!" This will encourage her to respond with more than just a vague reply; for a start, she'll be curious to know why you think that (which is good because a pattern then begins to take shape involving her asking you questions). With this assumption she has more to respond with.

Remember: a vague assumption = a vague response.

A lot of my students ask at this point, "But what if my assumption is wrong?" Which brings me to knowing where to go/what to do in that instance.

Just because you got the assumption wrong doesn't mean it should be seen as a conversation-killer. Remember that your main aim in those early stages of the interaction is to keep it flowing and to ultimately move the conversation on from those uncomfortable early stages. Moving it on is not the same as changing the conversation, so always remember that whatever her response to your assumption is – even if it's to confirm that you were wrong – it should always be seen as another hook, thus presenting an option to use another hook lead.

For example, let's go back to the assumption made about the girl who shops for bargains, but imagine for the sake of the example that she disagrees with your assumption and, in actual fact, only shops in more upmarket places like Harrods. Imagine for a moment that her response was, "You're completely wrong. I only go to Harrods, I never do jumble sales!" Here she has actually revealed more about herself than she realises. For example, she could be a total snob, or maybe she's 'Daddy's little rich girl', or perhaps she has a successful career which pays well. Maybe, on the other hand, she doesn't have a lot of money, but all that she does have is spent on clothes and jewellery that she can't afford. Try to find out, rather than just thinking, "Shit! I made a mistake!"

Remember to always work with what she gives you back, and see it as another piece of information to get to know her better. By the way, a lot of people who claim to be psychics use this technique:

I once went with my friend to see a supposed psychic. She wanted me to stay in the room with her and it turned out to be an interesting experience. The man held her hand with his eyes closed and began to say, "I see you are here because you have lost someone you loved very much."

She looked over to me and back to him with a bemused expression on her face. "That's rubbish, I haven't lost anyone I really love," she laughed, pulling her hand away.

The psychic replied instantly, "Tell me, have you ever really loved?"

"Nope, not really," she answered, looking annoyed (and probably wanting an immediate refund).

"This is a big problem in your life, and this is what will cause you unhappiness," he responded, completely calm and undeterred.

From that moment, she began to slowly get drawn in; she listened carefully as he continued.

"Your heart is cold because you have never loved."

"That's true," she replied.

And within a few minutes she was crying and revealing all her deepest emotions. The first assumption/guess/cold reading was a stab in the dark that was completely wrong – but it was forgotten about very quickly.

The so-called psychic did not start changing the subject, and he did not show any signs that he was under pressure because of his initial mistake; he simply used all the information he was given in response to the mistake he made to take the conversation further. (By the way, a lot of these fake psychics have degrees in psychology.)

Another technique you could use if the girl in questions tells you your assumption is wrong is called the 'response of intrigue', which involves you saying something like this: "Really? I'm surprised. So why do you prefer those kinds of shops?" This gives her an admission that you were wrong but tells her you're now intrigued enough to know more about her, as she's surprised you by being someone other than who you'd thought.

In the past I've made so many assumptions about people and sometimes I make sure they're purposely going to be wrong, because I can actually get more out of them than if I get an assumption right, simply by responding with a curious or intrigued expression on my face and saying, "Really? I felt sure that was the case. Tell me more." This then seems to distract the person from the mistake and gets them talking about themselves, revealing more about who they are and helping the interaction move on.

THE TWO-OPTION ASSUMPTION

This involves you making two assumptions about her rather than one, giving her two options to respond with. During the conversation, let's say you find out she likes to go to Greece for her holidays. Rather than assuming she might be interested in ancient history and archaeological ruins, you could say this instead: "From talking to you, I reckon you're one of two extremes." Her ears will prick up, mainly because people like to hear what others think of them. You could then continue by saying, "I think you either go to Greece purely for its beautiful and rich history – the ancient ruins, the mythological statues, etc – or you are totally, totally the opposite, going there just to lay in the sun, top-up your tan, drink cocktails in the bar and making a point of not doing any kind of historical touring or trekking at all. I'm certain it's definitely one or the other, not something in between."

Of course, she may be wondering why you're assuming she could be one of two such polar opposites. You could tell her that, going by what she's revealed about herself so far, you reckon she's an extreme person who doesn't do things by half measures, not an 'in-betweener'. It gives her the positive impression that you've been listening well and are making an effort to get to know her.

But then, what if she's neither, or a bit of both, I'm sure you're wondering? In this case, you can once again use the 'response of intrigue'. (It gets you out of a lot of mistakes, never underestimate its powers!) You can even admit that you felt sure she was one or the other, but that you're both surprised and interested to know about this other side of her character.

This hook lead is a great way to draw information out of her without actually asking a question. When someone assumes something about the person they're interacting with, the person usually responds as if it were a question even if it's not.

Assumptions are in the same category as cold readings, which I'm a massive fan of. Furthermore, the most important thing to remember is that, whatever her response to your assumption – even if she says you're wrong – you can still use it as another hook point to make a transition in the conversation.

SUMMARY OF THE NINE-HOOK LEAD SYSTEM

Obviously, it's much easier to explain how the system works face to face, as the tone of your voice, body language and facial expressions are very important in getting the desired effect of each hook lead across. But I've tried to be as detailed in my examples as possible.

One important reason why I teach the Nine-Hook Lead System to my students is that it encourages them to avoid getting into the question and answer pattern. All too often, men talk to women and get into this cycle of posing one question and getting an answer, then posing another and getting another answer, which feels like an interview process rather than a conversation and results in the girl making little effort in the interaction! But then, why would she? She knows that, whatever she answers, it is just going to be followed by yet another question. This, of course, leaves the man doing all the work.

Although the system does require a lot of work to begin with, it's more internalised, whereas a man who just asks a series of questions shows more external effort. When he doesn't use the hooks she's giving him a negative pattern is formed, usually by as little as asking three closed questions in a row, creating a questionnaire-like interaction.

When any psychological pattern begins to set in within an interaction, it becomes increasingly difficult to shift it to a more positive one. The Nine-Hook Lead System will free you from ever getting into those negative patterns in a conversation again, simply because it gives you options. The very fact that you're aware that every hook lead she gives you can take nine alternative paths is, in itself, enough to crush your fears of running out of things to say.

What the system does *not* do is alter your personality, but it does actively assist in enhancing it. I often draw an analogy with a good quality stereo system: imagine you have a CD with your favourite song ever on it. Imagine now that you put that CD into a really poor quality stereo system with terrible speakers, battered to death by years of heavy bass. You try to listen to the CD playing and, although you can just about make out your favourite song, the sound is muffled, has too much treble or too much bass and there's a really annoying hissing sound. As such, you struggle to listen because you know it's a great song, but eventually you get annoyed and give up.

Now imagine that you play your CD on a state-of-the-art stereo system, one of the newest on the market. Much to your delight, the music is perfect; you can hear every instrument in crystal-clear fidelity; the levels are exactly where they should be. Of course, the CD never changes; the song is still the same, but the equipment that was used to play the song the first time is useless compared to the second model. As a result, it changed the whole experience.

Using the Nine-Hook Lead System will not change your core personality but, much like the sound system, it will help you to show the audience – or, in this case, the woman you're talking to – who you are, what you're about, what you desire, what you find amusing. Remember: like the high-tech stereo which enhances the sound of an amazing song, the system is there to enhance the amazing personality you already have.

If you are just asking questions or are coming across as being slightly dull, it does not mean that *you* are boring. Just like that CD you chose to play, the song never changed; it was always a magnificent song but, unfortunately, it was let down by the equipment. Your personality is unique; no one else shares the same exact character traits as you. Do not let it down because of poor body language or poor conversation skills.

A lot of my students come to me saying that they think they're boring, and that's probably the reason why girls are not really interested enough to pursue a conversation with them. In response, I ask them if they think they're dull when they're with their friends, or people who know them well. Most of them say no, which answers the question perfectly.

Crucially, it's not their personality that's the problem; it's the way they express themselves, usually through poor body language and poor conversation skills. As a result, they end up revealing few or no signs of their truly interesting and unique selves – or worse, they hide their personalities behind a mask of nerves.

It's all down to poor marketing!

Men are usually too interested in asking a series of questions rather than sharing who they are. An interaction is always a two-way thing but, more often than not, guys will keep it headed in a one-way direction. They either talk too much about themselves, without listening to her (missing the hooks), or it goes the other way and they put too much focus on who she is, what she likes and what her opinions are.

So remember: use the system as a tool to assist and enhance the quality of your self-expression.

PRACTICE

After I've taught the Nine-Hook Lead System, my students often ask me how on earth they can be expected to remember all this. It's not as if they have the option of carrying the list in their pocket, and can pull it out every time they get stuck in a conversation. Obviously, trying to remember all nine options will result in information overload. So the advice I give is to pick just three of the options; I strongly urge Validation as one of the choices and Tasks as the other; the remaining hook lead I leave up to them to decide.

Next time you get into an interaction with a hot girl, and you get to one of those dead ends or uncomfortable silences, pick one of the three hook leads that you decided to use. Because there is less choice, you will be able to choose one almost instantly. The more you practice, the more you will notice that they become like a reflex, and this is when you can add another hook lead to make it four. Keep doing this and eventually you can add a fifth, and so on until your list consists of all nine. Choosing the right one for that moment and for that particular woman will become an automatic reflex.

You will be perceived as a naturally good conversationalist, and will increase dramatically your chances of being able to maintain the woman's attention longer than most other men can. More importantly, you'll have the ability to make the transition from the opener to a full-blown conversation smoothly and successfully.

• STEP NINE •
VALIDATION

The man who makes chemistry sees himself as a man of worth and because of that he sets his standards high.

HERE IS ONE of the most – if not the most – important lessons I can teach you. In my opinion, this point is not highlighted as much as it should be by other pickup artists, and yet it really is one of the main reasons why they manage to attract woman so well.

Every natural I know and every successful pickup artist always makes it a rule to place himself above the woman, seeing himself as the judge. He is the prize and he makes sure that, at some point during the interaction, he will get her working for his approval rather than the other way round.

Why is it like this? Let me answer this question with a question. Have you ever heard anyone say, "You can never please a woman"? Well, it's true! The man who tries to please a woman is constantly chasing a chimera that just moves further away the more he chases it. With this in mind, you need to stop and make a 180-degree turn in your perception of the situation; in doing so, *you* will become the one who needs to be pleased. And it is this – ironically – that is the very thing that will please her.

Women get a great deal of pleasure from pleasing men; they find a sense of worth in making him happy or proud of her. I admit that it's an old-fashioned idea, and something that us women have tried desperately to move away from. But the man who sets himself above her, demonstrating his high value and high standards to her, is a force to be reckoned with. It's also something we're attracted to. It's not very fashionable – or even politically correct – to admit to something like this, and on a personal level I've internally tried to battle it for years.

I've always considered myself to be a strong woman. Ever since I left school I've always made my own money, followed my own path and embraced the fact that women are becoming increasingly powerful – not only in relationships, but in all other areas of life and society. As such, anyone who knows me will describe me as an Alpha woman. But I've made a promise to be 100 per cent honest with you, the reader, and so I have to confess that I often enjoy pleasing a man. It gratifies me to know that I've made him happy, or that I've said or done something that he's impressed with.

However, this often causes me to question myself. *If I'm really as strong or as tough as I make out to be, then why do I still need a man's approval in certain personal aspects to make me happy?* I should point out here that when I say making men happy can make me happy, it's not as drastic as saying 'a man's happiness makes me complete,' but it's nevertheless still sometimes a difficult notion to accept.

But there are others out there, who are also typically strong women, who will admit to asking themselves this same question. One good example is my friend Lara. Lara is a 32 year-old who works in advertising, and is considered to be a very successful woman. She is one of my more 'Alpha' female friends, and believe me when I say she has more balls than most men I know. When researching for this book, however, I asked for her take on the whole 'pleasing men can make women happy' issue, and here is what she said (word for word):

"Yeah, it's something I struggle with too; it's such a taboo subject, especially in this day and age. I mean, look at me: I have a brilliant job, I'm more successful than most men I know, and I'm usually a lot smarter than them too! And yet, a man who makes me want to impress him is a huge turn-on.

"I like a man who looks me up and down and, after a pause, says something like, 'I like the fact you have that dress on, it's sexier than what the other women here are wearing.' A part of me wants to slap him, but another part of me feels slightly turned on. It's like I've made the mark."

"Why is that a turn-on?" I asked.

"It's kind of authoritative, and it shows me that he has high standards."

"It's very risky for a man to say something like that, though," I replied.

"That's true. He has to be really Alpha to be able to carry something like that off. But it doesn't have to be as obvious as that. A guy can show me that I've 'made the mark', so to speak, by showing his approval of things like my career. So many guys say stuff like, 'I really think it's great that you're such a successful woman,' blah blah, and it feels like they're kissing my arse. So if a man says something more like, 'I'm glad you're successful at what you do, it's important for me to speak to a woman who is strong-minded. I don't like weak women,' again that makes him seem like he has high standards, and then, for once in my life, I feel as if I have to keep making a constant effort to make sure that I keep up with those standards. It just makes him come off as more of . . . well, you know . . . a man. Do you see what I mean?"

"Completely," I answered.

Another example that helps illustrate this point further is that when a lot of my friends start dating guys, their appearances start to change very slowly. When I ask why they've started wearing that particular style or why they've been doing their makeup differently, they say, "My boyfriend likes it that way." It's even happened with me. I was once dating a guy who liked brunettes. Although he said I was beautiful, he'd often say, "You know what, Kezia, you look great but if you had dark hair you would be so, so sexy." So yes, I dyed my hair dark about two weeks later – and yes, it was purely to make him happy.

There are thousands of stories like these and they're extremely common, even amongst very strong and confident women. The urge to please a man seems so contradictory for women in this day and age, but, although we fight it, we nevertheless always seem to succumb to it.

The master seducer knows that his approval of her becomes like an itch that she needs to scratch.

If a man needs to 'approve' a woman before he asks her out, kisses her or sleeps with her, it makes him stand out from the rest of the men in her life. By doing this, he automatically sets himself apart from those too afraid to get her to qualify or validate herself to them. This type of man separates himself from the man who bends his opinions and standards just to keep the woman he's speaking to happy.

But be warned! There is a correct way to get a girl to seek your approval and, as with anything, there is also an incorrect way too. I will of course be sharing with you the correct way to do this, but first let me introduce to you the two types of validation you will be showing her.

POSITIVE VALIDATION

In relation to the Nine-Hook Lead System, this is the point where you show your approval based on the hook she's given you. Positive validation should always be given in a sincere yet slightly authoritative manner. Here is an example:

> You: What do you do for a living?
> Girl: I'm a teacher.
> You take a moment to think about it. At this point she wonders what you're thinking. (Most guys are by now asking her very boring follow-up questions, or immediately responding by saying how brilliant they think her job is.)
> You: That sounds cool. Most girls I talk to do something really boring that's centred on themselves too much, like modelling. It's nice to meet a woman who does something other than PR or fashion. A teacher? I like that. Tell me more about it. ['I like that' is optional, as in the early stages it can come off as a bit too arrogant.]

This is a good example of how positive validation should be delivered: you're showing the girl that what she said has pleased you, and you've done it by comparing her to other girls who haven't made the grade. This is more subtly powerful than you can imagine; the use of carefully selected words here says a lot.

Your expressions and mannerisms should also be subtle and should never display arrogance; instead, you need to give the impression that you're someone possessing 'inner worth', someone with high standards which need to be met in order for you to be truly attracted to the girl. (This is, of course, more appealing than a man with an uncontrollable ego.)

At the end of the example, you could also say, "I like that"; this is one of the key phrases when using positive validation. You are letting her know that she is ticking your boxes, which will effectively display to her that you have high standards which need to be met. (Remember that list I told you to compose in the pre-approach step? Time to use it!)

What is taking place in the woman's head here is a very subtle yet incredibly important shift in her perception of you.

She begins to see you as someone who is on her level or – even better – a level above her. Someone unwilling to accept whatever is given to them, or whatever happens to be on offer, because of the high value you place on yourself, your inner sense of self-worth and high standards.

When positive validation takes place a few times during the interaction, you set a pattern in her mind whereby she begins to feel attracted to the approval you're giving her. She also starts to genuinely listen to your points of views. Why? Simply because your validation seems so genuine. Think about it: most guys are just too happy to *love* everything she does; they're eager to please her just to get her to agree to go on a date, and so no matter what she says the response is always, "Really? That's so cool!" or, "I love that!" or, "That's so great!" As a result, she'll start to doubt the guy's sincerity and feel like she's getting hustled – how she feels when she goes into a shop and an overeager member of the sales team tells her she looks great in whatever she tries on. (Arse-licking for a sale, basically.)

However, provided it is done in the correct way, validation is key. I could write a whole book on just this one area alone. You will also need validation when overcoming 'bitch shields' (Step Ten) and will need to continue using it to a certain extent, even if you end up developing a full-blown relationship with her.

Here's a little secret about someone I know, who is fairly well-known in the pickup community (I haven't mentioned him in the book yet), and I'm happy to say that he is now one of the expert pickup artists on my team. I've seen him go from good to brilliant to one of the best PUAs in the world, and I'd say his relentless use of validation is one of the major reasons. He once told me, when we first met, that he wanted a really nice girlfriend who was good looking. It was a fairly common aspiration and I thought nothing more of it. However, a few months later he said he wanted a girl who was 'really hot', rather than just good looking, and apart from being nice she had to be very clever too. A few months after that, he said that his ideal girl had not only to be hot but tall with really good legs, and not only clever and friendly but also challenging and funny.

"You don't ask for much!" I remarked.

"Why should I ask for anything less than I deserve?" he replied.

"Well, you have a lot more requirements for your ideal woman now."

"That's because I'm improving," he smiled.

And his list is still getting longer and longer!

The funny thing is he still keeps getting exactly what he wants, and the girls that he only dreamed about in the past are now the ones that he's actively rejecting because his ideal has evolved so much. Whenever I watch him in action, I notice that he's always using a healthy amount of positive validation, but that he also uses a lot of the inverse too: negative validation.

The successful seducer does not bend his own reality in accordance with hers.

NEGATIVE VALIDATION

Negative validation happens when you disapprove of what she's said or done. I want to make it completely clear that it should preferably be used only after you've built her up with positive validation during the interaction.

This is a good moment to raise the issue of 'negs', or 'negging the girl'. These are little one-liners that a man says to a woman – usually a particularly attractive woman – which are intended to lower her value. Negs can come across as cheeky and, if the girl has a notably large ego, using them can have the desired effect. However, men are often using these on women who don't actually have a large ego to prick, thus leaving her feeling bad about herself. To help give you a better idea, here are some commonly used negs:

- You know, I just saw a girl wearing the exact same dress/outfit a little while ago.
- [to her friends] Is she always like this? How do you roll with her?
- You blink a lot.
- Those shoes look really comfortable.
- You are *sooo* cute, I'd adopt you. Put a little mat at the foot of my bed, you could sleep there
- Your nose wiggles when you talk! It's so cute! Look at it! There it goes again!
- Guy: I don't think we should get to know each other.
  Girl: Why not?
  Guy: I think you're just too much of a nice girl for me.
- [*Guy reacts as if she spat as she was speaking, and then says*] "Eww! Say it, don't spray it!"
- Guy: What do you do?
  Girl: I'm a model.
  Guy: Oh, like a hand model or something?

I've purposefully chosen a selection of different negs ranging from the cute and playful to the offensive; there are literally thousands which are posted on websites if you wish to find more.

I'm not saying that negs are the worst thing a guy can do, and they can help lower the value of an egotistical woman who's used to having all the guys drooling over her. They can also be considered cheeky, and cheeky is good; in fact, let me rephrase that and say that cheeky is *very good*.

But – and this is a *BIG BUT* – if the guy is too cheeky too early on in the interaction, he can come across as really annoying and might end up insulting the girl. There are occasions when the girl might have a great sense of humour and it can work out fairly well, but in my experience a lot of girls don't always see the funny side.

Recently, I met one of the top pickup artists, whose name I will not mention. Although he was successfully building up attraction with me, he ruined it by negging me way too much. The first couple of times were okay and, yes, they did help to tone down my ego, but by the third and fourth neg I started feeling self-conscious and unsexy. In the end, I made my excuses and went home. Since that encounter the guy in question has emailed me to explain but, unfortunately for him, it's too late.

The problem with using negs too much arises from the guy assuming too much. Guys automatically assume that the girl is going to put up her defensive shield, especially if she's beautiful, and so, based on their assumptions, they automatically try to neg her when it could be completely unnecessary. As a result, the girl is left either feeling bad about herself, embarrassed or annoyed – none of which can be considered a good start!

In the case of the pickup artist I met, I think he became addicted to putting me down and lost sight of the original reason he was talking to me (which was to sleep with me that evening). With this in mind, negs should be used in moderation; you should also monitor the woman's reaction to them because a guy can overdo this technique and the woman is left viewing him as a bully rather than being merely cheeky. However, if a man takes note of the woman's reactions and sees that she might be slightly upset about what he's said, he might understand when he's gone too far.

In my opinion, negative validation is a more powerful and advanced method of getting the girl to qualify herself to you than just using negs. The difference is that negative validation can be applied all the way through the interaction and even in long-term relationships, whereas negs are only good for the early stages of an interaction – after that, they have a definite tendency to wear thin.

If you're the person responsible for building her up, then you'll have the power to be the one who can break her down. Negative validation should start at the point when you notice she's becoming complacent about your positive validation; this is the very moment that you should switch tactics.

It's an advanced form of the push-pull technique. Imagine you're talking to her and she's feeling good (thanks to you and your positive validations); then she says something you might not be too impressed with. It could be something really small; maybe she laughs too loudly, maybe she starts swearing, or perhaps she says something about herself that you think is a bit stupid or inappropriate, or incongruent with the high esteem in which you had initially held her. For example:

You: Where are you planning on going this summer?
Girl: I really want to go to Spain, maybe Costa del Sol. They have great bars there with cheap alcohol.

You: *pause for a moment – pull an expression which voices disappointment (not like you're completely disgusted, but a little bewildered and/or unimpressed) – since you've been positively validating her the whole time, this will force her to ask you what's wrong – this is the start of her wanting to qualify herself to you.*

Girl: What's wrong? [*she notices your disapproving look*]

You: Nothing, just forget it. [*make it seem as if you don't want to offend her*]

Girl: Tell me! [*now she really wants to know*]

You: Okay, you promise not to get sulky or annoyed?

Girl: Yes, yes, I promise.

You: Well, it's just that I thought you would say something else.

Girl: Really? Like what?

You: Well, something more elegant or more cultured. You seemed really . . . look, forget it.

Girl: What do you mean? [*she's promised not to get sulky and she's trying her best to keep that promise*]

You: Look, you seemed like a really elegant lady, classy, exactly the kind of woman I like, so cheap drinks in sunny Spain is *not* what I thought you were about, that's all! But like I said, just forget it. [*again, you talk like you don't want to offend her*]

Girl [*looks a little upset, then begins to qualify herself*]: I do like other types of holidays too, I'd like to travel to Asia, I just thought Costa del Sol *would be fun*.

If she didn't care what your opinion of her was then she'd never try to justify her actions, or qualify herself to you. The reason she's doing this is because she wants to get back to that level of high esteem which you put her on; you're the one she has to go through in order to get that good feeling back.

It's important that you're aware of your tone and your words. You must make sure that it seems like you genuinely don't want to offend her. If you come across as rude or abrupt, then she might see it as a direct insult rather than a subtle sign or hint of disappointment.

Here follows one of the greatest examples of positive and negative validation working together. Let me take you back a couple of years:

Quite often, I frequent night clubs that attract celebrities, and it always fascinates me to watch normal women go temporarily insane when they spot a male celeb walk into the VIP area. Even if he's not good looking, the very fact that he's famous increases his attractiveness to levels which are off the chart.

One night in one of these clubs, I noticed not one, not two, but three famous movie stars from the USA. They were in London to promote a film and, as you can imagine, they had the pick of any girl they wanted.

Predictably, the women stood pathetically around, pouting and thrusting their large breasts (or small breasts) as close to the faces of the celebrities as humanly possible, while still stuck behind that all-important velvet rope. That little red rope was the barrier between them and paradise. It all goes to show just how fucked-up our perception of fame is.

A few of the girls began doing mildly erotic lesbian shows with each other for the benefit of the guys. (This, by the way, happens more than you think when a celebrity walks into the place, even a z-list celebrity.) I remember looking around at the time and thinking I didn't care what guy was in the club, I wasn't prepared to act like an unpaid prostitute. Instead, I opted to sit down and watch the ridiculous circus unfolding before my eyes. The stars were brilliant, and played their role perfectly; they were a class

*act, and if anything seemed more intent on talking to each other!
But every now and then they'd glance over at the girls and laugh
– which, of course, didn't offend them but only boosted their
hopes of getting picked even further. Eventually, they chose the
girls they wanted, numbering 15 if I'm not mistaken, which
amounted to five each – not a bad average!*

*As I sat and watched from the back, I began to look at the
other men in the club and felt kind of sorry for them. How could
they realistically compete with these stars? What chance did they
have with a girl who had her heart set on sleeping with a rich,
good-looking megastar? I don't really think men realise how
focused and determined the female of the species can be when she
has her heart set on something – whether it be a white wedding, a
family or, in this case, a night with a megastar. Subsequently, the
other men in the club looked grumpy, openly revealing their
jealous streaks by saying things such as, "He's just a rich prick,"
or, "His last film was bullshit."*

*Out of frustration, the other guys in the club started laughing
and pointing at the girls and the three stars in an attempt to make
them feel humiliated. Unfortunately for them, this only increased
the girls' desire to get into the VIP area.*

*Poor guys, I thought to myself. Do they really think insulting
celebrities will earn them attention?*

*Later on, I got into a conversation with one of the girls who
didn't make it into the chosen elite. (I say this with a heavy serving
of sarcasm.) She was a stunning blonde, with a stunning pair of
silicone breasts to match. But then again, there were plenty of
others there who looked like that.*

*"I've slept with countless stars," she boasted, adjusting her
microscopic dress. "It's only a matter of time before they notice
me and send for me to come over and join them." She added yet
another coat of gloss to her lips, obviously feeling very frustrated*

that she still remained on the wrong side of the velvet rope. "I mean, seriously, what's the point in sleeping with these nobodies when you can sleep with a film star?"

Of course, by this point her shallowness was more than obvious and her goals were short-term to say the least, but at least the girl was honest. As I listened to her sexual boasts about famous rappers and well-known sportsmen, I eventually grew bored. I was about to set off elsewhere in search of some mental stimulation, when along came Craig.

Craig was a fairly good-looking guy. He had fashion sense (good shoes!) and was clean-shaven, but was not what one would consider particularly outstanding. In actual fact, I'd say there were far more physically eye-catching men in the club that night. But, unlike the other guys, he showed no signs of frustration or malice toward the three celebrities who occupied the women's attention. Although he was aware of the situation in the room (only an idiot wouldn't have noticed), he nevertheless seemed detached from the mass frenzy as if he'd seen it a thousand times before.

This man was to demonstrate the art of validation to perfection; he was about to achieve the near-impossibility of distracting the blonde's attention from the megastars across the room and making himself the object of her desire instead, all within 20 minutes! And this is how he did it:

Craig came over and sat next to the life-size Barbie doll I'd been talking to. He laid back casually and lifted his leg up onto the table opposite us. The Barbie doll looked over to him as if he was a speck of dirt, looked back at me and rolled her eyes.

"I can't be bothered talking to this nobody," she whispered to me, "and if he stays here he might decrease my chances of getting picked." This girl was treating the whole thing like some relentless military operation.

"How come you weren't picked?" Craig asked with a smile, although barely looking at her.

"Excuse me?" she snapped, turning back to him.

He ignored the hostile tone of her voice. *"I think they have really good taste, these guys. I mean, they get to work with some of the most stunning actresses in the world – so, in my opinion, I think you're good enough to get picked by them."* His voice was gentle, the tone sincere and very matter-of-fact.

The girl was unable to think of anything to say back. It was obvious that she wasn't sure whether she was being insulted or complimented.

"Maybe you should try a different approach," he continued.

"Like what?" she hissed.

He thought for a moment. *"It seems that the good old lesbian dance routines get their attention, but everyone's doing that so it kinda loses its novelty a bit! Besides, I'm sure you would prefer to be one of their girlfriends to being just one of their conquests."*

"Maybe I'm happy just sleeping with them. Do you know how many of these stars I've been with?" she said, boasting again.

I was transfixed by the psychological game he was playing with her.

"That's pretty cool, but I know loads of women who've done the same and they aren't as cute as you. With your looks, coupled with the fact that you're obviously a very focused woman who's used to getting what she wants, I think you could be one of their girlfriends."

It was strange little game he was playing; although he was complimenting her, he was doing it in such a way that made him the judge; the judge of how she behaved and how she looked. He was also very clever at making it seem he wasn't particularly interested in having her for himself either!

"I guess I could," she said.

"You guess?" he looked surprised. *"If you just 'guess' you*

could then maybe you can't – I thought you seemed a very self-assured girl a few moments ago."

"I am!" she retorted, once again reapplying that dreaded lip gloss.

"Then why would you only 'guess' that you could be their girlfriend? Anyway, my ex-girlfriend went out with a famous footballer for a year. He gave her a car, took her on beautiful holidays, and he didn't hide her away either. He was proud to say she was his lady."

"What happened?" she asked.

"She dumped him." He paused for effect and sipped his drink before continuing.

"He was gutted to say the least. He thought she really was the one. He was sick of the easy girls; he liked a challenge, I guess."

He suddenly looked over to me, extending his hand in my direction. "Hey, sorry, I didn't see you there! I'm Craig," he gave a very cheeky smile, as though he'd dismissed the girl he was talking to just a moment ago.

Before I could say my name, the Barbie doll – in her very ruthless way – flicked her hair in my face in an attempt to hide my presence.

"I'm Jazmina," she smiled, taking his hand.

Now, let's break down what Craig had done. He'd played an advanced game of both positive and negative validation. He started by showing his approval of what she was doing and how she looked – although, in all likelihood, he probably thought she was just another groupie. He slowly built her up even more by saying that she seemed focused and confident, even more so than the other girls. But during the whole time he was showing his authority, not behaving in a needy manner.

After he'd smoothly reeled her in, he began to switch tactics by using negative validation, which he did by deliberating comparing her to other women – not to other women in the club (because he'd done that already), but women of arguably higher status. As this example shows, he'd first built up her ego to a certain degree (if it was humanly possible to build it up any more) and then purposely took it all away from her.

Of course, most people know that people who have big egos tend to hide equally big insecurities behind them. As if to confirm this, the Barbie doll subsequently found herself ignoring the megastars who'd been the centre of her universe only a few moments beforehand and qualifying herself to a guy she'd wanted to get rid of only a few minutes before!

Of course, he had no intention of helping her become the girlfriend of one of these celebrities; he just used the spiel as an opportunity to put himself in a more authoritative position whereby he could used validation to its full effect.

The moment he knew he'd not only distracted her from her original goal of getting a celebrity, but also hooked her in, was the moment he began to use a tactic known in the industry as the 'push-pull' technique – which, in my opinion, works very well.

PUSH-PULL TECHNIQUE

The principle of push-pull is about controlling a woman's emotions during a conversation. First, the guy will be nice with her to hook her in and/or will use positive validation, either of which acts as a 'pull'. Then, right after the woman has been pulled in, he demonstrates indifference or negative validation, which is of course the 'push' part (psychologically or emotionally pushing her away). This technique is effective because the woman never really knows if the guy is interested in her. As you probably know, it's human nature to want what we can't have! Furthermore, by consistently using the push-pull technique you'll begin to build a lot of attraction, because she'll start having to work for your attention or – even better – your approval.

Craig cleverly carried out this technique by dismissing her the moment he could see she was hooked in and was just starting to qualify herself; he chose this moment to use the 'push' aspect, whereby he looked past her at me and deliberately asked my name before hers. It worked beautifully.

Craig later went on to tell Jazmina how he thought that she wasn't really his type, and that he found women who teased him with a flash of flesh to be far sexier than those who put everything on display. He told her how she'd look incredible in a long black dress with her hair up, and by doing this he deliberately created the opportunity to touch her (kino), whereby he gently took her hair and piled it up while inspecting her neck.

This guy was brilliant – he was actually giving her advice on how to improve herself. Most would just stand there drooling and tell her how hot she looked.

Oh, and by the way, this story has a very happy ending. The last time I saw Craig, he was leaving the club at around 3am with Jazmina, the Barbie doll, holding onto his arm – and her friend was on the other one.

SUMMARY

Positive validation involves showing your approval of what she has said, or what she looks like, what she is wearing, how she dances, how she behaves, etc.

- It should be done in a sincere manner, but also delivered unapologetically.
- It must never sound needy.

- It is a perfect way to show her that you have high standards, and therefore enjoy the luxury of being fussy when it comes to women.
- It should be used to show her that you that you have high values.
- It should be used when you want to achieve the 'pull' part of the push-pull technique.

Negative validation involves showing your disapproval or disappointment over something she has said or done.

- It must be said in a sincere manner.
- You must make it seem as if you genuinely don't want to offend her too much.
- You should use it when you want to achieve the 'push' part of the push-pull technique.

Now that I've explained to you how to use both positive and negative validation, they will play a major part in ensuring that you achieve the next step.

• STEP TEN •
BITCH SHIELDS

The man who makes chemistry sees the potential in every type of woman and welcomes the challenge that even the most difficult ones bring.

NOW WE MOVE smoothly onto the dreaded 'bitch shields'.

A lot of my students hate this part, but it's a key issue which needs to be addressed. Let's start with a question I'm often asked: "Why should I learn how to destroy bitch shields? If she's a bitch then that's her problem, I'll just walk away if she's horrible." Well, firstly, if you refuse to learn how to destroy bitch shields, then you'll automatically cancel out a large percentage of your targets! (Harsh but true!) Remember that even the nicest girls have some form of shield that they use from time to time; it doesn't automatically mean that she's a cold, heartless bitch or that you'll never get anywhere with her – that's why its called a 'bitch shield' and not a 'bitch core'.

The master seducer understands that if her 'bitch shield' goes up then it can be systematically brought down.

Imagine that you're in a club and checking out a group of hot women. Unfortunately, you're not yet aware that the group has its resident bitch (or possibly just a woman with a bitch shield). She will be the outspoken one, and she'll make it her mission to ensure she is the one you have to get past in order to get to the others.

Blissfully unaware, you confidently open the group and try to talk to one of the girls that you've had your eye on. Then, unfortunately, along comes the bitch! She will, at some point, turn her attention to what you're doing and will purposely stand in between you and her friend. So what do you do in this situation? Well, if you haven't yet mastered the art of destroying bitch shields, then the chances are that you'll simply admit defeat and surrender your opportunity of getting to know the girl you've been looking at across the room all night – all because of her hostile friend.

But if, on the other hand, you have mastered the art then you can choose the next option, whereby you spend no more than five minutes of your time destroying the shield of the girl standing in the way of you and her hot friend; as a result, you'll not only get the attention and respect of the girl but also the acceptance of the rest of the group.

WHY DO WOMEN HAVE BITCH SHIELDS?

Here are three of the most common reasons:

Reason One: Put yourself in our shoes and understand that women get hassled *a lot*! When we go to a club or a bar, we are hassled even more. Years of this can make our defence shields come up very quickly indeed, before we have the chance to get to know the man who wants to talk to us. Unfortunately, whenever we've decided to be nice and friendly in the past, guys have usually taken this as a clear indication that we would like to have sex with them. As a result, we find that the guy starts hanging around too much and by the end of the night becomes like an unwanted mosquito, buzzing around us non-stop. This type of man never even stops to entertain the notion that maybe we're just happy to politely socialise for a few minutes.

This is precisely why we sometimes choose to act cold and unfriendly without thinking about it. We've unfortunately experienced way too much of the dreaded 'mosquito factor' in the past and so, in order to save ourselves – and him – the time and energy, we automatically put up a bitch shield.

Reason Two: Sometimes, we have a bitch shield just for the simple reason that we've had a bad day, and the next man who dares approach us will be automatically in the firing line whether he deserves it or not!

Reason Three: We sometimes put up a bitch shield in order to help us find the strongest of the Alpha males in the vicinity.

Women will sometimes use a series of putdowns on the man as a way of testing him. They will carefully assess his responses and reactions and, if he's seemingly able to defeat her and withstand the negativity, he automatically becomes worthy of respect. (As you're now well aware, a man must be respected before he's considered attractive.) In contrast, however, if he fails to defeat her bitch shield or becomes notably upset because of the little tests, then he'll be considered too weak to earn her respect and automatically ruled out.

This type of bitch shield is also known in the pickup industry as a 'shit test', which literally translates as the woman giving the man shit or some attitude to test him with. I've included shit tests under the heading of bitch shields because the method and techniques of destroying the latter are virtually the same.

Below are the three main points you need to learn:

DESTROYING BITCH SHIELDS

Getting Detached

The first thing you must do is become detached from your emotions, which is a crucial point to remember.

Whatever you do, don't get angry. I know at some point you may just want to shout at her and tell her, "You're an ugly bitch!" If you're like me and have a short temper, then I understand that doing this might give you a temporary sense of satisfaction. But, ultimately, it will not get you what you want. It will bring your state right down and could potentially ruin the rest of your evening.

If you show your anger or lose your temper, she will respond by either laughing at you or shouting right back at you, causing a big scene which every other woman in hearing distance will notice. Consequently, they will avoid going anywhere near you for the remainder of the evening! If you get emotional, she will have seen it as a victory; she will relish the fact that she got to you, that she has the power to change your upbeat mood. With this in mind, you should *never* give anyone the power to change what state or mood you're in.

A good way of detaching yourself from your negative emotions when encountering a woman with a bitch shield is to alter your perception of her. For example, try to see her as either a 'little comedian', a 'precocious cheeky child' or a 'bratty little sister'. (Make sure you use patronising terminology when you do this.) This will produce better results than seeing her as a 'mega bitch' or a 'terrifying woman'. In addition, look at her bitch shield as an amusing source of entertainment rather than a barrier to be reckoned with!

Our perceptions of people can have a huge influence on the way that we interact with them and so, by shifting the perception you have of the woman, you'll not only find that your anxiety decreases but that you'll be less inclined to feel anger or frustration.

Learning How to Spot and Destroy 'the Pattern'

After you've successfully detached yourself from unwanted emotions, you can still find yourself getting caught up in a 'negative psychological verbal pattern'. Being aware of when a negative pattern in the interaction is taking shape, and being able to change it, is the second step you need to master in destroying women's bitch shields.

Here is an example of an interaction between a man and a woman who has her bitch shield up and is purposely creating a negative psychological pattern:

Guy: Hey, I need a quick female opinion on something.

Girl: [*aggressive tone*] What?

Guy: Can you suggest a present for my female friend? It's her birthday and I need to get her something really nice. I have a budget of £50. Any ideas? [*He remains calm, happy and detached.*]

Girl: Why the fuck are you asking me?

Guy: [*remaining calm*] Because you look like someone who has good taste.

Girl: Why the fuck do I look like someone who gives a shit? Do you think I've got time to waste on you?

Guy: Well, uh, I just thought . . .

Girl: Are you trying to chat me up?

Guy: No, I just wanted to know if . . .

Girl: Look, what have you got to offer apart from this lame chat-up line?

Guy: Pardon?

Girl: Where are you from?

Guy: London, I live just near . . .

Girl: What do you do?

Guy: I'm a financial trader.

Girl: What's that?

Guy: Well, it's someone who works on the stock market. It's a great job and . . . So what do you do?

Girl: Look, why don't you stop wasting your time and go to someone else?

This is a typically negative pattern that a girl with a particularly defensive bitch shield might choose to set. Although the guy has kept his emotions in check and is refusing to get angry with her, he's unfortunately still making the fatal error of getting caught up in her pattern. This is what she did in order to create a negative pattern in the interaction and how his response only fuelled it:

- She fired questions at him and he answered, even though she was obviously only doing this to make him jump through hoops.
- She interrupted him with a further question, which he again answered.
- She controlled the frame of the interaction by taking the conversation wherever she pleased, regardless of what he wanted.
- She made a point of never answering his questions, and he accepted this.
- She forced him to explain himself and, in doing so, simultaneously got him to qualify himself.
- She made him jump through hoops with no reward at the end.

Here is an example of how the same situation can be improved if a man deliberately disturbs the pattern she wishes to set:

Guy: Hey, I need a quick female opinion on something!

Girl: What?

Guy: Can you suggest a present for my female friend? It's her birthday and I need to get her something really nice. I have a budget of 50 quid. Any ideas? [*He notes from the tone of her voice that she's going to be hostile; therefore he's aware that he must destroy her bitch shield as soon as possible, so he immediately takes control of the frame and interrupts her before she answers.*]

Guy: Now, before you answer, take your time to think about it; I'm looking for something original.

Girl: Uh . . . some shoes? Look, why are you asking me?

Guy: That's a good question. Would you believe me if I said it was because you look like a woman of good taste? [*He playfully smiles.*]

Girl: Yeah, but you're just trying to chat me up.

Guy: At last, I'm talking to a straightforward woman!

Girl: What? [*She looks confused but is intrigued.*]

Guy: Why do you look so shocked? Hasn't a guy ever described you like that before?

Girl: Uh . . . yes, no . . . I don't know . . . Yes, they have said it before.

Guy: I prefer a straightforward woman who speaks her mind, better than all those sweet butter-wouldn't-melt-in-my-mouth girls.

Girl: Yeah, I know what you mean. [*She finally breaks into a little smile.*]

Guy: At least with you I can now get some honest advice on

this gift issue. Now, stop changing the subject, will you? So you mentioned shoes – what type?

Girl: Uh . . . well, what type of shoes does she like?

Already the guy is completely controlling the frame. Although he answers her questions, he always makes sure that he validates them first. He shows his approval of what she has asked him and therefore immediately places himself in a higher position than her. In this example, he even goes on to approve her whole general attitude (comparing her to 'sweet' girls who don't impress him as much as fiery women).

With regards to the answers and responses which he chose, she did not expect any of them at all. This continually forced the pattern of the conversation to go in an unforeseen direction and, as a result, gave him more control over the interaction. You need to throw her something unexpected out of leftfield, which will force her to start working harder to keep up with you. Anything that can avoid a negative pattern is always a bonus.

One of the trainers I've worked with was particularly good at doing this. He would go up to a woman who looked Scandinavian or Northern/Eastern European and ask her where she was from. If the girl responded by asking, "Why?" in an aggressive or confrontational tone, he'd simply smile and say, "Well, I was looking at you from afar and I couldn't work out if you were from North Korea or South Korea." The woman would nearly always laugh at his response and, in doing so, automatically lower her shield – simply because she was not expecting this particular response.

VALIDATE, VALIDATE AND VALIDATE!

If a woman is putting up her bitch shield, validation is the last thing she expects you to respond with. Using it will disturb the negative pattern she wanted to get you into. Whenever I'm in my bitch mode and a guy tells me how much he loves it, I automatically realise that being a bitch will not bother him and that, not only can he handle it, but he also finds it slightly amusing. So I come out of bitch mode fairly quickly!

I once had a student called Lewis who specifically wanted to learn how to destroy bitch shields. Lewis was good in all the other areas, such as conversation skills, building rapport and creating sexual escalation, and his stage was very strong (all six columns were perfect). However, he still struggled with his particular sticking point.

"I just get so scared when women start being bitches," he confided in me.

And so, for a period of 16 hours spread out over two days, we worked obsessively on bitch shields. I have to admit that, when we did role-play, I really did push him to his limits. (My bitch shield is known to be particularly vicious!) But, when he began to understand and apply the techniques, he slowly began destroying my shields until eventually he was ready to go and put his newfound skills to the test.

I knew exactly the place to take him, a spot where plenty of Alpha females liked to go. It was a bar in the City of London, which all the powerful female lawyers and City traders frequent after work. Perfect!

The bar was nice and busy and, just as I'd expected, there were lots of women dressed in power suits, all enjoying glasses of fine wine. The aura of sheer confidence these woman possessed gave them an almost Amazonian quality that would frighten even the most Alpha of men!

I immediately spotted a group of five attractive women in the centre of the room. I gave the nod to Lewis and off he went.

He opened them well. He was high-energy and in a positive state of mind. I noticed that his body language was strong and that his voice was confident.

"Hey, ladies," he began. "I need to get your opinion on something."

Suddenly, one of the women raised her hand in a 'Do not come any closer!' manner.

Lewis stopped.

All eyes were now on him.

"You can only have our opinion if you buy us all a drink," she said with a big Alpha smile on her face.

The other women laughed, and the outspoken woman – who was obviously the leader of this pack – looked at the other girls triumphantly.

I sat and watched. I knew exactly what he needed to do next – we'd been through similar scenarios in role-play. The problem was that if he showed any sign of weakness at this point, or if any of the columns of his stage (points of body language) fell apart, then it would be game-over.

But, thankfully, he did as he was taught.

He looked the woman right in the eye, smiled (bordering on a laugh) and said in a firm but friendly tone, "I'm not going to buy your friends a drink."

Just as she opened her mouth to respond with what most likely would have been a cutting putdown, he interrupted her. "I'm going to buy you a drink."

You could see the girl was a bit confused.

"Why so shocked?" he asked, smiling.

From where I was sat, I could see her eyes darting quickly to the side and back again as she tried to think of a response.

But, before she could speak, he interrupted her again. "I'm going to buy you a drink because you were the only one out of all *your friends who was outspoken enough to ask – but on one condition . . ."*

She stared at him curiously. "What?" she eventually asked.

"On the condition that I choose the perfect drink for you. Believe me, it's not that pink cocktail you're drinking! Just trust me. Waiter!"

It was brilliant. The woman smiled – and something as small as this can be a clear indication of when a girl has let down her bitch shield. Of course, she accepted the drink that Lewis chose for her and they got talking.

The other girls were impressed with the way Lewis had tamed their leader and, within ten minutes, he was very much accepted into the group.

Funnily enough, he ended up getting the 'bitch's' number – who turned out not to be such a bitch after all. Lewis told me a few weeks later that she was absolutely lovely, and had a dry, wicked sense of humour that he adored.

So, let's summarise what Lewis did to destroy this woman's bitch shield:

First: He kept his composure. He showed no signs of panic, nerves or anger, which are the most common signs that men show when under pressure in an interaction with a bitch, or facing a bitch shield. In other words, he managed to detach himself from all negative emotions.

Second: Lewis used validation almost right away. Remember, positive validation is your secret weapon here, even when the girl in question is clearly being a bitch! And yes, I know and understand that the last thing you want to do is pay her a compliment when she can't even be pleasant – but remember, positive validation is *not* a compliment; it is only a sign that you've approved of something she's said or done.

In this particular scenario with Lewis, he let the woman know that he felt that she was entertaining him and that her bold demand was not only something that he had no problem in handling but was actually something that he found rather attractive.

Third: Lewis successfully took full control of the frame of the interaction right at the very beginning. He interrupted the woman and kept responding with something that she was not expecting, forcing her to abandon her negative pattern and follow his own.

Lewis's perception of the women, he told me later, was of a small group of 'cheeky girls', rather than a large group of tough 'Alpha female lawyers', which helped decrease the initial anxiety he was experiencing just before he opened them.

FINAL REMINDERS ON DESTROYING BITCH SHIELDS

- Keep your composure whilst ensuring you do not get emotional about the situation.
- View her as a 'source of entertainment', a 'bratty kid sister' or a 'precocious child', rather than a 'mega bitch', an 'evil woman' or a 'horrible person'. Our perception of people can have a huge influence on the way in which we interact with them.
- Be aware of your stage; remember that all columns must remain strong, especially facial expressions and eye contact, which are usually the first two to start breaking down under pressure.
- Validate, validate and validate! This is your secret weapon.

- Be aware of all the patterns she tries to set up; even if it seems easier at first to let her carry the conversation, it will be hard to make the transition to another level if she has been controlling the frame from the beginning.
- Remember that when she is in her 'attack bitch' mode, she is only asking you questions so that she can use the answers you give her (irrespective of what they actually are) as a weapon to embarrass or deter you
- Understand that, in order to disrupt a negative pattern, you need to add the element of surprise and do or say something unexpected; this forces her to surrender the pattern she wants you to follow because she is too busy following a new one – your own.

• STEP 11 •
SEXUAL ESCALATION

The successful seducer understands that women do not want to be 'picked up' – but they love to be seduced.

THERE YOU ARE, sitting at a party with a hot woman you met only two hours before. After a fair amount of time getting to know one another, you both feel very comfortable and relaxed. You notice that your legs are gently brushing against hers and that she's laughing at your jokes, even when they're not that funny. You're also aware that, every time you go to the restroom, she loyally saves your place on the sofa next to her. You seem to have her complete undivided attention and, even when people at the party have tried to distract her, her attention always comes back to you.

Yep, all the signs are there – she clearly likes you; you know you're not imagining it. But, despite this, you wake up the next morning alone in your bed.

You're lying there alone not because she rejected you or because you imagined the whole scenario, but because you did not make a move! Consequently, for the rest of the week, you feel totally shitty about yourself. However, you do reap some comfort from the fact that you still have her number, so you ring her up but – guess what? – she makes it clear that she's not interested, but still happy to be friends (which only adds salt to your wounds). To make matters worse, you find out that she's going on a date with one of your friends who was also at the party; you know, the guy who took the initiative and made a move on her after you left the party with only her telephone number (the consolation prize). And, when you think you've reached the pits of embarrassment and rejection, you find out she actually liked you more than your friend, but just thought that you weren't attracted to her – either that or you were gay.

What a great morning after the night before!

You might have experienced similar scenarios to this one, surrendering the opportunity to sleep with – or at least kiss – a beautiful woman. There are a few reasons why so many men out there make this mistake and consequently miss the boat. In this step, each of the most common reasons why men do not create sexual escalation will be addressed.

By introducing you to the art of sexual escalation, I'm going to help you conquer this very common sticking point so that you never have an excuse to miss – or avoid – those future opportunities again!

WHAT IS SEXUAL ESCALATION?

Sexual escalation is when you take the interaction to the next and final level, the seduction level. It is the point where you show her that you're attracted to her, and that you'd like to see her as more than just a friend. It's done by changing the energy of the moment, which can be achieved through altering the tone and rhythm of your voice and your eye contact. Changing the mood can also be achieved by slightly altering the conversation to one of a more sexual nature.

WHY ARE SOME MEN USELESS AT SEXUAL ESCALATION?

Along with approach-related anxiety, the escalation stage is the part of the interaction that men fear the most. At first he's relieved that he got past the initial point of possible rejection, which is of course the opener. Once he's passed this, he might manage a smooth transition to a full-blown conversation with her; in doing so, he will have built up a great rapport with her and made her feel totally comfortable. But, just as everything is going well and he's starting to relax and enjoy the conversation, he suddenly realises he needs to create a sexual escalation. Once again, he finds himself facing yet another point in the interaction with a possibility of rejection.

With this fear bubbling away beneath the surface, he either postpones that moment until it's too late or decides not to do anything about it at all, instead waiting patiently for a miracle. (A miracle, in this case, would involve the woman taking his hand and telling him in no uncertain terms what she wants him to do to her.) In fact, the amount of fear that men tend to generate around this part of the interaction can be even greater than the kind they experience when approaching a girl, purely because rejection at this level is a lot more personal because she's actually got to know him a little. Consequently, because he might have done well so far in the interaction, he will literally do all he can to avoid ruining it. As such, there's a good chance he'll decide to play it safe and not create any sexual escalation at all.

Men who do this fool themselves by saying things like, "What a great evening, and if I'd really wanted to I know I could have slept with her!" Of course, this is a complete cop-out.

Imagine for a moment an athlete running an important 100-metre race. Imagine he's in the lead and has been consistently doing really well, but then, at 70 metres, he suddenly stops and says to himself, "I know I could have won, that's good enough for me," walks off the running track and goes home. Surely you would think it was completely ridiculous? But ask yourself this: what's the difference between the athlete who refuses to cross the finishing line, for fear of the small chance that he won't come first, and the man who avoids sexually escalating his interaction with a girl he likes and is doing well with, just in case she might say no?

Always close the deal.

The second reason men avoid sexual escalation is because they leave it too late. They remain in the comfort stage for too long and, as a result, the relationship becomes a friendship. Because of this, he starts feeling that if he tried flirting with her now, or showing any sexual interest whatsoever, then it might come across as being 'inappropriate' or 'sleazy'. (In my time as a teacher, I've found that men have a huge fear of being perceived as 'sleazy' or 'creepy'.)

The third reason for avoidance is simple: he avoids sexual escalation because he doesn't know how to do it. Maybe all of his previous conquests have happened as a result of when he had little or no control over the situation, e.g. when he and the woman were both drunk, or high, and ended up literally falling into bed together, or maybe when the girl took control and had to practically drag him to the bedroom.

But the other, most common explanation that men have for how they managed to sleep with a woman in the past is 'chemistry'. (Remember the message I gave about 'chemistry' back at the beginning of this book.)

This is the reason a man gives when he has no explanation at all; he doesn't know how he managed to sleep with certain women in the past, and so whenever he tries to recall the events of that successful interaction he'll only say, "the magic was there," or, "everything just clicked," or the classic vague statement, "it all just kinda happened." This is of course completely unhelpful, and is exactly why he has struggled to recreate those results again since.

Remember, in the first step I described how everything can be broken down and taught, understood and replicated. Do not look at your past conquests as a result of magic or chemistry; instead, remember that chemistry is a sensation which comes as a direct result of attraction – and attraction can be created.

Those nights when you were successful happened for a reason, and the reason is that you managed to somehow create an attraction; you must look back to your success stories and break them down step by step.

From now on you will not:
- end up getting stuck in the friendship zone for longer than necessary.
- need alcohol to deaden your fears, or numb the uncomfortable feelings you get during the act of seduction, because there will no longer be any uncomfortable feelings to numb.
- be obsessed with not coming across as 'creepy' or sleazy'.
- allow the fear of rejection to stop you from making a move.
- avoid sexual escalation and be content with the fact that you 'could have' if you'd tried.
- sit back and hope that the girl will take control, or that you will attract a man-eater who'll drag you into bed with her.
- hope that the magic and chemistry somehow creates itself out of thin air.

Instead, you're going to be in control of sexual escalation. What's more, you're going to eventually love this part more than any other part of the interaction!

THE THREE STAGES

I've divided this section into three stages, so that I can explain the process as clearly as possible.

The Introduction Stage

This is at the beginning of the interaction, the stage where you're delivering your opening line. It's also the stage where the initial introductions to one another are still being made.

Your level of energy in the introduction stage should usually be fairly high. But of course this depends on the situation and the circumstances. For example, let's say that you're at a bar or club where the overall energy of the place and the people is generally very high. You decide to open a set of three girls who are all in high spirits. Your energy will have to match theirs, or be higher than theirs, in order to distract their attention. On the other hand, if you were to approach a girl in the daytime who was sitting in a quiet coffee shop, reading a book, your energy levels would not need to be as high but would still have to be (at the very least) equal to hers.

However, after a while you should make sure that the high energy state you had when you approached her in the beginning tones down a little. Usually, it should start toning down when you start focusing your attention on just one of the girls at the club, rather than all three or, in the case of when you're approaching a girl on her own, when you've distracted her from whatever she was doing before and taken the conversation to a deeper, more personal level. Obviously, if you were to maintain a high energy state it would come across as ridiculous and may give the impression that you're overenthusiastic (a common mistake) or, even worse, high on drugs.

The point here is that you must begin to decrease the amount of energy in your state, and start talking to her on a one-on-one level rather than to her and her friends as a group. In the case of talking to a girl on her own, when you've managed to get her full attention you've reached the point when you're taking things into the second stage.

The Comfort Stage

This is the second stage of the interaction. At this level, you should be happy to know that half the battle is won: you've managed to get away from the introduction stage by making a transition smoothly away from the opener (hopefully by using the Nine-Hook Lead System) and, in doing so, have also managed to distract her from her friends, or whatever she was doing before you approached her.

During this stage, there might be some touching (kino); maybe you've touched her on the arm a few times or, even better, maybe she's begun to touch you. However this has panned out, the whole point of this stage is to build comfort. What better way to know if the person you're talking to is comfortable in the interaction than if they actually let you touch them, or they touch you? Obviously, the last thing any of us wants to do is to touch or be touched by someone we're not comfortable with. Seeing how she reacts to your touches is a reliable indicator of whether she's comfortable with you or not.

(By the way, this stage is still completely non-sexual, so when I say 'touching' this doesn't mean intimately stroking her thighs or the back of her neck.)

At this point, the interaction can go one of two ways: either it can start to get flirty and then lead to sexual tension, possibly a kiss and then further; or it can remain in the comfort stage forever and, by the time you've plucked up the courage to kiss her or ask her out on a date, she gives you the mortifying line, "Let's just be friends."

The reason why the latter happens so often is because the guy has remained in the comfort stage for too long. And so, even if the woman was attracted to him, she hasn't been given the opportunity to show it or act upon it. Finally, as the moment where sexual escalation could have occurred moves on, she starts to see the interaction more as a friendship rather than anything sexual.

Although it's possible to create another chance, it does become tougher the longer it's delayed.

The Seduction Stage

This is the third and final stage of the interaction. Some people describe this as where they start flirting, others regard it as where they create sexual tension, some call it the moment when they start heating up the situation, some say that it's the point where they can make their move and others that it's when they're getting her in the mood, or turning her on.

I believe it's all of those and more; it's the stage in the interaction where you present her with the idea that something wonderful, something filthy, something hot and something naughty can happen between the two of you – without actually saying it.

In order to seduce a woman, you must understand that making her feel comfortable and relaxed is only part of it, as is getting her to like you and feel an attraction towards you. (These are things that should be focused on in the comfort stage.) Seduction is about letting the woman know you desire her and want her, and giving her the opportunity to show that she desires or wants you too.

Seduction must ultimately make the woman feel sexually desired. I cannot stress this point enough, and it must be done in a completely unapologetic manner. Women do not respond well to a guy who is embarrassed or uncomfortable with the fact that he is attracted to her; this immediately makes him come off as unsure and doubtful, which are very unattractive traits in a man. A man who shows the woman that he really wants her is more attractive than the man who shows her that he might perhaps like to sleep with her (if she doesn't mind, that is).

There are some men out there who are naturals at seduction, and I've met them; these men can be fairly bad in all the other areas, but when it comes to the seduction stage they do really well. However, most men do unfortunately find this area to be the most difficult. If this applies to you, then remember: anything that one person can do, another can learn.

I'm going to give you the two main points in relation to your body language that you need to master in order to create sexual escalation. As a result, it will help you fulfil the seduction stage.

The Voice

When you create an escalation, you must first start by being aware of what your voice is doing. Firstly, the pace or rhythm of your voice must slow down; you can't create a seductive moment if you're talking fast. The best way to achieve this effect is simply by putting extra pauses in between most of your words. A lot of my students ask me what they should be saying during the seduction stage, but I tell them what I'm telling you now: don't worry too much about what you're talking about; you don't need to be poetic, or use romantic or sexual terminology, to turn a woman on. Sexual escalation is not about what you say but all about how you say it. The power of words cannot match the power of energy. Of course, telling a woman that she looks stunning can have a positive effect, but it will not create sexual tension if it's said in a normal, everyday manner. The volume of your voice must decrease too, which will then force her to move closer to you to enable her to hear what you are saying.

The Eyes

I want you to imagine that there is a triangle on her face, like the picture below:

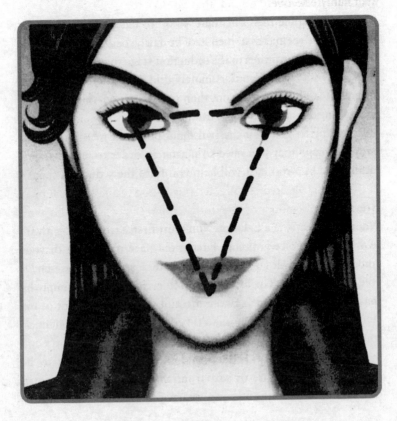

Start by looking at her right eye, move slowly to the left and then down to her lips. Hold your gaze on her lips for a second longer than necessary and then back to her right eye. This gives the illusion that you've just noticed her beauty and you have a sudden desire to kiss her. This technique has proven to be very effective.

Our eyes tell others so much about the way we feel. Looking at a girl's lips for a moment longer than necessary is very sexual, and is a clear sign that you have an urge to kiss her. Keep in mind that you can use the triangle on her when she's talking, which is also incredibly effective.

Using the triangle technique with your eyes, coupled with alternating the rhythm and tone of your voice, will help make the transition from comfort stage to seduction stage. By making these adjustments you are literally changing the mood and energy of the interaction, creating sexual tension.

Making the necessary alterations to eye contact and voice also gives the effective illusion that the girl has slightly bewitched you. Up to this point you've been chatting to her more like a friend than someone who's attracted to her. By momentarily making her feel sexually desired, you're actively changing her perception of you and the mood of the interaction. Importantly, the word 'momentarily' is the key here, and you need to remember this: a woman does not want to be overwhelmed with the fact that you suddenly want her. (Whoever said that women are difficult?)

I will now teach you the 'dipping' technique, something that has not been taught by any other trainer or pickup artist.

THE DIPPING TECHNIQUE

Imagine if you went straight from the comfort stage into the seduction stage without any transition; if she's not ready then this can be understandably overwhelming, even if she's attracted to you.

Often we, as women, are attracted to a man, but the moment he suddenly comes on too strong makes us feel as if we're faced with an ultimatum, as if we're being cornered. Plenty of times I've felt an attraction but, as a direct result of him coming on too strong, I've decided to adopt the 'thank you, but no thank you' attitude; if he'd warmed me up before going in for the kill – by flirting and creating sexual tension – he would have given me the chance to actually enjoy the process and the opportunity to flirt back. One brief moment of wondering whether a man is attracted to you or not can be thrilling, too.

So, rather than exiting the comfort zone completely and going straight into the seduction stage, you instead need to dip in and out of the two stages which will slowly build up the sexual tension, so that you don't make the mistake of overwhelming her and are better able to assess the situation.

EFFECTIVE DIPPING

The next time you're confidently talking to a woman and are still in the comfort stage, I want you to enter the seduction level for only two or three seconds. Slow down the rhythm of your voice and make the triangle sequence with your eyes. When the three seconds is up, go right back into the comfort stage as if nothing has happened. What this does is allows her to momentarily experience the fact that you desire her; if you do it correctly, she won't be aware of what you've just done on a conscious level but, subconsciously, she will feel a slight change in energy though not yet enough to react to it.

You need to keep repeating this process slowly, as the interaction continues, entering the seduction stage more frequently and also remaining within the comfort zone for longer and longer. Three seconds becomes five seconds, which becomes eight seconds and so on; this is a great way to get her psychologically prepared for the moment that you actually kiss her, and allows her to become used to the idea that you desire her.

The early stages of creating sexual escalation are probably the most difficult, so please, if you're feeling very nervous about this part then practise on women that you're *not* attracted to at first.

ASSESSING THE SITUATION

Dipping in and out is also a fantastic way of assessing the situation; if done correctly, this technique is 100 per cent risk-free, in that at no point will she reject you. However, that doesn't mean she will jump into bed with you either, but that you'll not go through that moment of rejection – when she suddenly looks at you, takes a step back and says that heart-sinking line, "What are you doing?" The reason this cannot happen with the dipping technique is because the shift in energy you're creating is so subtle it will be near to impossible to notice it (providing it's done correctly).

In the early stages of implementing this technique, you're purposely getting her used to the idea of the interaction moving slowly into one of a more sexual nature. But if she's not yet attracted to you, or is not ready to move with you to the seduction stage, she will show you some very subtle signs.

If you've been transitioning between comfort and seduction in a discreet manner, as advised, then she too will respond discreetly; therefore, if she's not comfortable with how the interaction is going, especially when you're momentarily in the seduction stage, she will display any one of the following:

- She leans back from you slightly.
- She begins shifting her eye contact more frequently to the side, for longer than necessary.
- She folds her arms across her chest.
- She brings her glass between the two of you.

These are very subtle signs, and she won't even be aware that she's sending them out. She will not consciously feel as if she's rejecting you – and how could she? Remember, she's not even aware of the dipping technique that you've been using on her.

There are, of course, some other signs she'll be showing you if she's comfortable with the changes you're creating. Below are some of the signs you need to look for whilst creating a sexual escalation, in order to know if she's comfortable with the direction in which you're heading:

- She breaks eye contact but only to look down and then back up again, almost as if she's bashful.
- She carries on touching you and lets you touch her too.
- She is making her very own 'triangle' when looking at your face.
- She moves closer to you.

Dipping slowly from one stage to the next is a great way for you to assess the situation and work out whether you need to concentrate more on the comfort stage. If you try the technique again and she's still showing any of the signs that say she's not ready, you might be able to determine that maybe she's just not interested in you. But you'll be able to find this out without her actually saying anything, or even being aware that you were assessing her. This means that you can still go and chat up one of her friends. Why? Because if you've performed the technique correctly, she will not be aware that you've even tried it on with her and won't be telling her friends how you made a move on her first.

WHAT NEXT?

So let's say the signs she's sending out are all positive ones; this means she's comfortable with what you're doing. As long as she continues to show these positive signs you should continue dipping in and out of comfort to seduction until the intervals between the two stages become less frequent.

Eventually you're fully in the seduction stage, and this is when you kiss her. Don't suddenly get scared and go back to comfort. Think about it: if she's responding with clear indicators of interest, then there really is nothing more to be nervous about.

When you're ready to make your move, look at her lips as if you're about to kiss her, look back up at her eyes and, with a very subtle knowing or cheeky smile (the emphasis here again is on the 'subtle'), slowly move forward for the kiss.

As previously mentioned, you should practise this first with a woman you're not particularly interested in. My students feel less nervous when doing it this way, and when they see the results they can achieve they feel confident enough to try it with a woman they *really* like.

FLIRTING

The dipping technique can also translate as 'flirting'

Women LOVE flirts. This is because they play with our emotions by momentarily turning us on, rather than full-blown sexual escalation whereby we can be so overwhelmed that we feel forced to respond in some way. Flirting is more of a tease that allows us to enjoy a 'could be' moment, without being forced to act upon it.

A male flirt flirts for his own pleasure as much for the woman's. He enjoys being a flirt, and likes to leave the woman second-guessing. When we encounter a good flirt, we're constantly presented with the question: "Does he like me or is he just flirting?" Of course, this serves to fuel our curiosity, and as a result the man seems more intriguing.

When a man flirts with us, we're made aware of his sexual side and his playful nature too. This subsequently creates a feel-good factor and is precisely why women enjoy the company of a flirt.

Just make sure that you do eventually create a sexual escalation with the woman you want, who shows clear indicators of interest while you're flirting.

· STEP 12 ·
CLOSING

IN THE PICKUP community, a 'close' literally means closing or sealing the deal at the end of an interaction with a woman. There is the 'number close', which refers to getting the woman's number; there is the 'kiss close', which refers to kissing her; and finally there is the 'F close', which means sleeping with the woman. (To put it a little more sweetly!)

Some are known as 'solid closes', which means that the woman probably really likes you and the chances that you will see her again are very high. In the last couple of years I've also heard the term 'Facebook close'. Obviously, kissing or sleeping with the girl are the most solid type of close a man can obtain, whereas an 'email close' or Facebook close are the weakest.

If a girl offers you her email then there is less chance you'll see her again than if you'd slept with her. (Emails can be more easily ignored than phone calls.) The most common type of close is the number close and, at the very least, this is what you should be aiming for if you're chatting up a girl in the daytime, at a bookshop, a café or in the street. Obviously, going for a 'kiss close' is a little more difficult (but not impossible).

If a woman gives you her number in a daytime scenario, then

it's usually more solid than if she gives you it in a nightclub (where you should aim for a kiss close). Women feel more exposed and vulnerable when they're approached in the daytime, so if you manage to secure a number from her that means you've managed to build up enough comfort and trust to help her get over the initial vulnerability she was experiencing.

Circumstances in a nightclub are slightly different; women tend to feel a lot more relaxed and in high spirits, and therefore a lot less vulnerable. Obtaining a telephone number from her while she's in a nightclub is more likely to be flaky than if she'd given it to you in the daytime. Remember that if she's drunk a few shots of tequila; this might indeed help you to number close her, but the next day, when you try to call her, minus the general sense of euphoria she might not be so keen on the idea of seeing you again. She may have given her number out to a few people the night before, and is now probably regretting it. This is why the kiss close is far more solid in this kind of scenario.

Since we've already gone through the whole sexual escalation process, we will not be looking at ways to obtain kiss closes and F closes (the information is all in Step 11); instead, we're going to focus on two points:

- How to get her number.
- How to make sure she doesn't flake out when you call her.

GETTING A NUMBER AS A RESULT OF DAYTIME OR DIRECT APPROACHES

You can actually go for the number close when still in the introduction stage of an interaction. Obviously, if she's waiting for her bus or is in a rush to get somewhere, you might not have the time to build up to the comfort stage. If time is limited, then of course it's better to seal the deal then than not at all. This is sometimes known in the community as 'direct game', meaning that you go straight up to a girl and almost immediately let her know that you think she's cute and would like her number. For example: "Hey, I just had to come over and say hi, and tell you that I think you're beautiful!" or, "I would be gay if I didn't come over to you and say hi!" These are just two examples of direct approaches, or direct game.

If all goes well from that point, then a man can number-close a woman literally within a minute of meeting her, but the majority of the time women will not give out their details when asked too early on. If you want to try direct approaches and direct game, then you must understand that the key here is your energy, your state of mind and, as always, the strength of your stage.

I know from personal experience that, when I'm walking in a busy London street, if a man tries to approach me with low energy, he'll usually fail to catch my attention or distract me from what I was doing. On the other hand, if he has high energy and the delivery of his opener is believable and his body language strong, then the chance of me agreeing to give my number is significantly higher.

However, when using direct approach, if you do achieve a number close it's more likely to be flaky unless you act upon it very soon after the interaction. (We'll go into more detail about this in the next step.)

But if you're not restricted by time and you have the opportunity to move the interaction from the introduction stage to the comfort stage, you should try to steer the direction of the conversation towards your goal – which is, of course, getting the woman's number. Such a conversation can be based around building a connection with the woman on an external or superficial level, in order to try to establish some common interests you might share. Get her to talk about what she likes doing when she's not in the office, or what type of cuisine she likes; these are two of the most easy subjects to help make the transition to a number close.

Let's say, after a little digging, that you find she likes Italian food (although most girls usually say Japanese). You could respond in a few ways, the most obvious being, "I like Italian food too, we should have lunch sometime." If she likes you then it'll be fine, but if she still hasn't made up her mind then this second option might be better. Rather than just telling her you like Italian food too before asking her to dinner, try adding a small element of playful challenge:

> **You: I like Italian food. In fact, I *love* Italian food, but I bet you haven't tried the best Italian café in London.**
> **Girl: Actually, I know some really nice Italian restaurants.**
> **You: I'm sure you do, but I know one that sells the best cappuccinos in Europe, even better than the ones in Italy. [*You then make it look like you've suddenly had an idea out of the blue.*] I tell you what, I'm going to take you there sometime for one of their cappuccinos, and if you admit that they're the best you have ever had, then you have to pay, but if you can find better then I will pay. Deal?**

The same can apply when asking her out to the cinema. Why not add a small challenge or a playful 'neg', such as: "Hold on, before we can go to the cinema together and watch this movie, I need to ask you something important. Do you prefer to sit in the front row or the back row?" Always respond with the opposite of her choice. "In that case we can't sit next to each other, I only sit right at the front. But don't worry, we can discuss the film afterwards."

These little added negs/teases/challenges make the situation a little less tense. You're conveying the message that the date will be playful and fun, rather than seedy and intense. (We women really worry about this!)

When it comes to actually getting her number, I find the best way to begin this is by telling her you have to leave. (You should always be the first one who has to leave the interaction, which will automatically give you the upper hand.) Firstly, you must pick the point where you've reached the pinnacle of the conversation; this is the moment when you've made the strongest connection with her, either emotionally or verbally. It's the perfect moment to stop, simply because it will always be followed by a lull which makes it a lot harder for you to reach another high in the interaction, subsequently making it more difficult to number-close. When you stop at that moment, you'll automatically be leaving her in a state of wanting more. Try saying something like the following: "Listen, I'm sorry, but I have to go, I'm meeting some friends and I'm being really rude keeping them waiting. But I've really enjoyed our conversation; we should continue this another time."

You're demonstrating to her that you have an active social life by mentioning how you have to see your friends. You also said that you enjoyed 'our' conversation rather than 'the' conversation, which plants the suggestion that the interaction was a pleasure for *both* of you. Lastly, you said that 'we' should continue the conversation, which is far more powerful than saying, 'I would like to,' or, 'it would be nice,' or, even worse, asking her permission by saying, 'can we?'

Here is the second part of what you should say: "Here, put your number in my phone and I'll drop you a text in a week or so." As you're telling her this, take your phone out of your pocket and hand it to her casually; this is giving her a task – you're telling her to put her number in your phone rather than asking her to do so.

Remember the Nine-Hook Lead System? I said that if you used the 'task lead' a few times during the interaction, then you'd find it a lot easier to get her to comply with the final task (putting her number in your phone). The other important point is the fact that you said, "I'll drop you a text in a week or so," which is very relaxed and casual, and will stop her worrying whether you might start constantly ringing her or become too hot and heavy too soon.

Sometimes women get last-second doubts when handing over their details, which is why I give my students a further technique to add onto this, which I call the 'nickname number close'.

THE NICKNAME NUMBER CLOSE

Once you've handed her your phone, you must discreetly assess her reaction. If you can see she's about to hand it back and say she's not sure, or that she doesn't know you yet, then it's at that exact point that you must interrupt her: you have to do this before she's actually refused to give you her number. Simply put your hand over the phone, as if to stop her from entering it, and say, "Hold on, before you put in your number, I want you to do something." At this point she will suddenly be distracted from what she was about to say. You then say, "I want you to make sure that you put your number under a nickname," at which point the woman will question why this is, and you respond with, "I can tell a lot about people from their self-imposed nicknames," before taking your hand away from the phone and smiling cheekily.

This will be another task for her and since it's a playful one she should be quite willing to comply. But also, using this technique will suggest that she's already agreed to give over her details. Never underestimate the power of assuming – like the nickname close, good salespeople use assumptions all the time. You go into a store to possibly buy an item, and you notice that the good salesperson will not ask if you actually want to buy it but will instead ask how many you want – making you believe you've already decided on it and are now in the process of working out how many you need!

MAKING SURE YOU DON'T GET A 'FLAKY NUMBER'

So you've rung her up and continued where you both left off. You've invited her to go see that movie that she told you she really wanted to see, but, unfortunately, she says that she's busy and suggests that another time would be more convenient. So you text her a few days later but she doesn't respond. You then try and phone her again, but she ignores your call. This is when the woman has flaked out on you. But why? Well, there are many reasons; let's begin with the three most common:

- She's had time to think about it, and has subsequently told herself that she doesn't really know you; she's feeling that meeting with you might be a bit weird, or even unsafe.
- She got back with a boyfriend she was having problems with at the time you asked for her number.
- Because of your high energy and ability to connect with her on a superficial or external level, she was sold on the ʾidea of giving you her number. But the high of that moment unfortunately subsided about four hours later.
- She got a better offer.

These are the most common reasons why a woman finds excuses not to see a man she's given her number to – but this need not be the case. If you don't have a restricted timeframe, simply build up a deeper connection in order to ensure she doesn't flake out on you. As I explained in Step Five, if you achieve 'deep connection' with a woman before getting her number then the chances of her flaking out are greatly reduced. Of course, if you obtained her number within a tight time constraint and were therefore only able to make a surface connection, then there's a chance that she will flake out on you. Again, this is why I cannot stress enough how important and beneficial it actually is to make deep connection.

When a woman feels that you've seen a side of her that she mostly only reveals to people she trusts, she'll then automatically place you in the same category; this will eliminate the excuse that she doesn't trust you enough to see you again.

Another reason why making a deeper connection will make her want to see you again is that women usually enjoy talking to someone at this level; although we enjoy light, unimportant chit-chat, there is something about having a deeper, more meaningful conversation which captivates us and makes us open up. We often complain that men are too worried about getting emotionally close to a woman, so if you show her a hint of this deeper, more sensitive side to your character during the initial interaction she'll be more drawn to the idea of seeing you again. Again, the key here is trust, which reiterates why the comfort stage is so important; if you can achieve this, she won't be sitting at home later questioning your intentions, wondering whether you're a weirdo or not.

Getting a woman's number by using a direct approach while still in the introduction stage doesn't automatically mean she'll flake out on you; if she gives you her number quickly, this can be a sign that she's a woman who is drawn to excitement and the possibilities of the unknown, and may agree straight away to see you again as she is the kind of person who lives for the moment.

ONLINE ROMANCE? NO WAY!

If you only managed an email or Facebook close, then you must do everything possible to stay away from getting the 'chatting only online' or 'online relationship' scenario. This is becoming more common, and an increasing amount of my students are asking for advice on what to do with a woman they've been chatting to online for weeks, or even months. Getting away from an online relationship is tricky, to say the least. Unfortunately, when we talk online with someone for too long (even someone we've actually met and exchanged details with in real life), we get used to the idea that it'll remain an online relationship that will realistically never make the transition to anything more. It also has a lot to do with the fact that we can be more confident, wittier and funnier when hiding behind a computer screen, so the idea of meeting someone again in the harsh light of reality is not very tempting.

My advice is: get her number as soon as possible and phone her! Get her used to hearing your voice, rather than just seeing the words that you typed flash up on her screen. Get the interaction away from the computer quickly. Arrange to meet up with friends, even if it's at a nightclub. The main point is to end the online relationship, otherwise you might find yourself stuck in it for months, even years. And the longer you remain in it, the harder it will be to make the transition from it.

• STEP 13 •
THE PHONE CALL

The man who makes chemistry understands
the importance of timing.

AS MY STUDENTS start progressing and obtaining the numbers of the women they approach on a more regular basis, it's natural for one or all of the following questions to come up:

- When should I contact her again?
- What should I text her?
- When I phone her what should I say?

Of course, every woman is different, and so it'd be misleading for me to tell you the exact moment you should call her or the words that you should say. But at this stage, I'll give you the general rules of what works and what does not.

Women usually find that the guy makes contact after the initial interaction either too soon or too late. If you met her in the daytime and used direct approach to get her number, then (and I know this may come as a surprise) you should really call her that evening. This is due to the fact that you obtained the number as a result of creating a 'moment'; the whole interaction was spontaneous and full of energy, which, although powerful at the time, quite rapidly decreases after you part company. With this in mind, if you call her in the evening that feeling that you created between both of you will probably still be fresh in her mind. You need to act upon it before it fades, to ride the wave.

Why not invite her to see a movie that evening, or to go to a club or a bar? Try to get her to bring a friend or two, and get some of your friends to come along too. Whatever you want to do, remember: if you wait too long after a direct approach and a rapid number-close, then you might find it hard to get her back into that positive state of mind. You began with an out-of-the-blue scenario, so you should continue it that way.

Aside from obtaining her number through a direct approach, the general rule is that you should call her or text her on the third day after the initial interaction. Whether you've only got her number, kissed her or slept with her, the time delay remains the same. So why three days? Well, when women meet, kiss or sleep with a guy, a part of us does want him to phone the next day; yet if he actually does that, although it makes us temporarily happy and our ego is nicely boosted, we also then know for sure that he really likes us. And if a guy shows he's too keen too soon, he immediately loses his power. The initial delight that we get from the phone call starts to deteriorate pretty quickly; we see it as a sign that he's hooked and it implies that we need not make too much effort.

A woman needs to be kept in limbo sometimes, which will ensure your phone call is much more appreciated than if you'd called straight away. It also demonstrates that you're busy and have other things on your mind besides women. And that, of course, makes us appreciate the phone call all the more.

THIRD DAY LOGIC

So why the third day and not the fourth or fifth? As stated above, on the first day after our meeting with the guy we'd like him to call, but are not too bothered if he doesn't; by the second day, we're starting to wonder why he hasn't called but are not yet at the point of feeling rejection; by the third day we're contemplating whether to call him ourselves or not, and have probably already spoken to one of our girlfriends about it. With this in mind, if you call by the evening of the third day – or, at the latest, the fourth day – you'll then have reached her just before her uncertainty turns to anger. And this is very important. When a man keeps a woman waiting too long, his phone call might be met with an icy cool response or, even worse, she might not even pick up. You want to avoid the stage where she actually becomes angry with you, and the third day is the right moment.

WHAT TIME?

Yes, I really do get asked this question! But to be fair, it's a fairly good one, because there are always those people who always call at the wrong time. It's as if they know the moment you're just about to board a train with your hands full of luggage, or when you've just settled down to watch a movie. I once told one of my friends who had this habit what times she should actually call me, and it sorted out the problem pronto!

Obviously, one woman's work schedule differs to that of the next. If she's a model, a stripper or just a general party girl then she's not going to be too happy about you calling her at 11:00 PM due to the fact that, in all likelihood, she will be too busy with work to talk – which may then lead her to question whether you even remember from your initial meeting what she does for a living, and the hours she keeps (assuming you covered work during the interaction). However, as a general rule, most women finish work at around 6:00 PM and, aside from Fridays and

Saturdays, will probably have eaten by 7:00 or 8:00 PM and caught up with all their soap operas by 10:00-10:30 PM.

My friends and I agree that between 10:00 and 11:00 PM is the best time for someone to call us. We're usually surfing the internet or watching a TV show at this time, not interested in anything in particular or probably just contemplating whether to go to bed or not. So I'd recommend you to call her sometime from Monday to Thursday, between 10:00-11:00 PM. But what if you got her number on a Tuesday? Okay, let's make an exception – call her on the fifth day, which lands on a Sunday. Unless you really want to invite her out to a club on Friday or Saturday night (the third and fourth days) – but be warned, she's most probably made arrangements and so will probably say she's too busy anyway.

THE PHONE CALL

When ringing up a woman for the first time, I find that it creates a better impression if you have some activity that's audible in the background. Try and call her when you're out – obviously not while you're in a really noisy bar or club, but maybe when you're with people or out in the street. If you're at home, put on some music or the television, though don't use them as a way to make it seem like you're outside; you should just make sure you're not in a silent room while making the phone call.

It's better to have some noise in the background than calling her with nothing but silence. Nine times out of ten, the first phone call after the initial interaction can start out a little uncomfortable; the woman might even feel a little shy, and so getting the conversation going might prove tricky. If you have some background noise, it helps distract from those potentially uncomfortable silences and the general awkwardness of the conversation.

The other reason why having noise can be beneficial is that, when people are talking to each other on the phone, they immediately build up a picture in their heads of what the other person's wearing, what they're doing and where they are. If there's some activity going on in the background, she'll assume you're not just lying on your bed or sitting on your own in a dark silent room, with nothing better to do. She'll have a more positive image of you out and about or with friends, being busy and sociable.

Of course, when she's more relaxed and the awkwardness of the situation has subsided, you should then either turn down the music/TV or go somewhere quieter. (Make sure that you make a point of this.)

One other reason to have background noise is as good cover to prevent the other potentially embarrassing moment when she says that she's too busy and can't talk to you. In this instance you can simply pretend that you can't hear her. Just say you'll call her later when you're somewhere quieter.

Remember: girls love to talk on the phone; we would transform it into an Olympic sport if we could, but make sure you don't slip into the role of being her 'phone buddy'. At the end of the phone call, make sure that you arrange a date.

· STEP 14 ·
GOOD GUYS VS. BAD GUYS

The master seducer is irreplaceable.

HERE'S A WELL-WORN cliché for you that you've undoubtedly heard before: "Nice guys finish last." So is this true? Well, yes, it is – but not in the way that you might imagine.

One question I'm commonly asked is, "How do I stay away from being Mr Nice Guy all the time?", followed closely by, "How do I prevent myself ending up as just her friend?"

The 'let's just be friends' scenario is commonly a result of being Mr Nice Guy and delaying or avoiding sexual escalation. (Mr Nice Guy would never dream of trying to kiss a woman for fear of offending her, so the two usually go hand in hand.) If you feel that these sticking points sound even vaguely familiar, then you might be suffering from this very common syndrome. But before I can teach you how to stop coming across as the nice guy all the time, we must first understand a few things about this issue in its entirety as it's more complex than it sounds.

First, let's establish who this 'Mr Nice Guy' actually is and who we're comparing him to. The term 'nice guy' is often misinterpreted as meaning the 'good guy' or the 'kind guy', and what my students are often surprised to learn is that, in actual fact, the 'nice guy' and the 'good guy' are at opposite ends of the spectrum.

In this section, I want to ensure you are not marketing yourself as the 'nice guy'. Yes, you read that right – I said 'marketing' because, as you'll soon find out, that's what's really happening here.

In addition, I'm also going to share with you the reasons why women are attracted to that clichéd 'bad boy' character and, furthermore, why they hate the nice guys. But, perhaps most importantly of all, I'll free you from the need to go back to being Mr Nice Guy again – and all of this *without any alteration to your true character*.

But, before we dissect the nice guy, let me introduce you to the two other guys who are very much part of this equation.

THE BAD GUY

- This character has a 'love them and leave them' attitude towards women.
- His motto is that old cliché, 'treat them mean to keep them keen.'
- He purposely plays on the woman's insecurities or weaknesses.
- He won't avoid sexual escalation.
- He is unreliable, meaning he doesn't call when he says he will or will be late for a date; this keeps the woman in a state of limbo, whereby she doesn't know where she stands in the relationship or whether he really likes her or not. And as she sits by the phone, waiting for his call, she puts herself at his mercy, which ultimately hands all the power over to him.
- He creates an element of drama which, although it upsets her, draws her in like a moth to a flame.

These are the bad guy's traits – but these alone are not enough to make women attracted to him. There are actually two fundamental reasons for the attraction:

- **He presents her with a challenge.**
- **He is proud of who he is.**

Women often strive to be the one who enters his world and literally saves him from the dark side that has been a part of his life for so long. (It's another cliché, but it's true!) By her fulfilling this role she hopes that, in return, he will forsake all other women just for her.

Very many women want to be the person responsible for melting the bad guy's icy heart, and the first woman to tame him. To achieve this would make her feel special, the only one from his (very long) list of women good enough to mend his wicked ways.

On a personal level, my friends and I have all dated bad guys. At one time, I honestly felt that I'd be strong enough and he'd love me enough for him to change his ways. I fooled myself into thinking that underneath that cold, hard exterior was a kind and loving man. (Actually, there was a sensitive soul underneath it all. But, looking back, it was never worth all the effort it took to get to it.) I believed that he'd eventually not need any other women to satisfy him – because I was the one who he'd been waiting for deep down. I was so caught up in the challenge I'd set myself that I was unable to see clearly. A lot of women that I've discussed this with realise that very often they were attracted to a bad guy for similar reasons.

Women believe that securing love and affection from a bad guy means more in terms of its value than if it were from a nice guy; this is because the bad guy *supposedly* never falls in love, which ultimately makes it seem unattainable and thus more appealing.

The second fundamental reason as to why a bad guy increases our levels of attraction is because of the pride he has in who he is and what he believes he stands for. Think about it: men have grown up believing that the bad guy is the cool guy. *Scarface* is rated as one of the most universally loved films by men and (especially) adolescent boys, who as we all know are extremely impressionable. And who is the main character in that movie? It's the ultimate bad guy, Tony Montana.

Posters of this movie have been hanging in the bedrooms of young men since the 1980s, and continue to sell well to this day. Montana has become an antihero and a template for the hardcore bad guy. Every single day, men are emulating this character and others like him, but on a much smaller scale of course. Tony Montana has the ultimate 'Who gives a fuck?' attitude, he's ruthless, cold and definitely a master of the motto, 'Treat them mean to keep them keen.' Taking this into consideration, is it any wonder that men feel good when they're thought of as the bad guy by the opposite sex?

The bad guy prides himself on who he is, boosted by the fact that his friends usually encourage his behaviour. For example, when he boasts to his friends about how he cheated on a girl with her best friend, or how he managed to manipulate a girl into sleeping with him, his friends will usually high-five him or congratulate him on his achievement. And so his pride is constantly being reinforced, whether it's by the media, his best friends or the women he is successful with.

The bad guy shows his pride and is totally unapologetic for who he is. Because of this, he demonstrates a personal strength. And what have we previously highlighted as a woman's ultimate need? Yes, you got it: strength.

I can hear you saying, "That's all very well, Kezia, but I'm not that guy at all. In fact, I don't even want to be him, regardless of whether he gets women or not. I respect women and have no interest in hurting their feelings or treating them like dirt." My answer to you is this: I said that there were *two* types of men who attracted women, and if you feel the bad guy's traits are contradictory of the beliefs you hold and your general view of women, then you'll be able to identify much more with the character traits of the second guy in this equation – and fear not, because this guy gets the girl just as often as the bad guy; in fact, let me rephrase that and say he gets *even more* women . . .

THE GOOD GUY

- Makes the women around him feel good.
- His motto is, 'Leave people better off than when you meet them.'
- Has a sense of his own high value.
- Has high standards corresponding to his own sense of high value.
- Has no intentions of hurting the girl.
- Respects a woman but demands respect in return.
- Can be a lot stronger mentally and emotionally than most other men.
- Is notably open to the idea of falling in love.
- Does not avoid sexual escalation.
- Uses 'unapologetic vulnerability' (rather than Mr Nice Guy's apologetic variation).

But we have still not touched upon the two most important reasons why women are often attracted to the good guy. These are:

- He presents her with a challenge.
- He is proud of who he is.

Sound familiar? Although the bad guy and the good guy are complete polar opposites, they actually unite in the two fundamental reasons as to why they attract women so much. Let us start with how the good guy presents the woman with a huge challenge – even bigger than that of the bad guy.

Firstly, the good guy has an immense amount of pride in who he is and what he stands for; he is not ashamed of the fact that he cares about people, that he respects women, that he wears his heart on his sleeve. And, because of the fact that he's unapologetic, he subsequently becomes extremely appealing in the eyes of a woman. Not only that, but the good guy clearly realises his own worth; this is not to say he's egotistical, but only that he understands that a man like him is hard to find.

The good guy is a clever character who understands perfectly well the law of supply and demand. He knows full well that there are a lot of women out there looking for a good man who will love them and be true to them. This means the demand is huge. He acknowledges that there are quite a lot of bad guys on the market, and that there is a flood of nice guys – but a noticeable lack of good guys, thus making the supply very limited and subsequently increasing his own value (a bit like the UK's housing market). This knowledge, combined with the fact that he feels pride in who he is, presents the woman with a huge challenge: in order to keep a guy like him she has to reach his high standards, which are a luxury the good guy can afford, purely because the rest of the guys out there offer no real or serious competition to him.

Do not make the common mistake of thinking that, just because the good guy has respect for women, he's a pushover; this is not the case at all. In actual fact, the good guy is not afraid to challenge the woman he is interested in, nor will he avoid teasing her or voicing his opinion, and he will definitely not avoid creating a sexual escalation with her. The good guy is by no means some kind of monk; he is as sexual as the bad guy, but the difference is that he will respect the woman the morning after and not make her feel used, or like a cheap slut. It will be at this point that she probably starts to realise he's the type of guy she would like to spend more time getting to know – and the kind of guy worth keeping.

And now we move on to the last character in the equation. He is the most common of the three figures and the main focus of this chapter.

THE NICE GUY

- He will never challenge the woman.
- He will never poke fun at her or tease her.
- He is a fan of the nervous laugh.
- He avoids sexual escalation.
- He often gets into the 'friends zone'.
- He is happy to hold her coat and bag for her while she goes off and flirts with other men.
- He always agrees with what she says and does (even if he doesn't really).
- He hardly voices his opinion if it contradicts hers.

The two main characteristics the nice guy is lacking are the two most important when attracting women – which the bad guy and the good guy both hold in abundance.

- The nice guy presents no challenge to women whatsoever.
- The nice guy is apologetic for who he is and shows no pride.

The above reasons, as I'm sure you've figured out by now, are why women are not attracted to the nice guy. All too often, the good guy is put into the same category, which is a huge mistake to make. It must be made clear that the two characters have nothing in common!

The nice guy = bland, forgettable, replaceable.

Get that into your head: the good guy is irreplaceable, one in a million, whereas the nice guy is the complete opposite.

Ask yourself this: do you consider yourself to be bland, forgettable and replaceable? The answer, I'm sure, is no. You know full well that you have a lot going for you, that you have a personality that can't be found in anyone else. You have your own views, your own opinions, your own dreams and fantasies, your own fears and sense of humour, your own memories and anecdotes, your own hopes and desires – yet you may sometimes choose to hide all this and instead market yourself as bland, forgettable and replaceable, rather than unique and special as you are.

If anyone described me using any of those three negative adjectives, I'd personally find that a far greater insult than if someone called me a bitch; at least that would mean I'd made some sort of impact, that I offered a level of vibrancy – regardless of whether it was negative or not!

Always remember: you are not bland, forgettable and replaceable, so don't market yourself that way! Would a well-known brand like Coca Cola market themselves as dull and replaceable? Of course not! They market themselves as the best on the market! The only real choice! A brand above all others! Maybe you should start applying this simple logic to your method of marketing?

WHY DO NICE GUYS CONTINUE TO BE 'NICE'?

So why do men continue to market themselves as the nice guy, when being *that guy* will always get them nowhere? There are two possible answers to this.

The first answer is simple. Men who do not understand or cannot master the art of attraction will often stay in their comfort zones. This means that when they get into an interaction with a woman they'll choose to avoid making any impact at all as they're so scared of getting a negative reaction. So, what do they do? They opt to play it safe; they stay in their comfort zone and, by doing so, automatically market themselves as the nice guy, without realising that, if someone does not make an impact on another human being, they will then be instantly labelled 'bland forgettable and replaceable'. I deliberately repeat these terms for the reason that I want you, the reader, to understand what the nice guy really is; I want you to be repelled by him so much that you never *become* him again!

There is another reason why men market themselves as the nice guy. Let me tell you a story about a friend I used to have, who we'll name Oliver.

Oliver and I had been very good friends since primary school. He was one of the funniest, most intelligent and charismatic men I ever knew. He would blow me and our other friends away with his intellect and have us in stitches with his dry wit. He was really a great guy, due to his personality, his kind and caring nature, his incredible fashion sense and good taste in music. This guy was a catch! The problem was, however, that none of us could figure out why he never seemed to get many women – well, not nearly as many as he should have been getting. I confronted him about this one day and asked him why it was.

"I really don't know," he replied. "If I know a girl likes me

then I'm usually okay, but if I'm just approaching women, I seem to get no further than the first ten minutes, and then she either wants to be my friend or she just walks off."

We scratched our heads and tried to work it out: every woman who'd ever really gotten to know him always fell completely head over heels for him, but the ones who didn't (according to Oliver) never even seemed to give him a chance. With this in mind, I looked him up and down to make sure that I wasn't imagining that he was a hot-looking guy – as I suspected, it wasn't my imagination.

Oliver then suggested that I come out with him when he next went to a bar, and that I should try and listen in on conversations he'd be having with women; he thought that maybe I'd be able to spot something he was unaware of. It was a good idea, and I immediately agreed.

Soon after, Oliver and I went to a bar in west London. There were quite a few good-looking women there, but most of them were just average, everyday. Nevertheless, Oliver chose to go and speak to a woman who, at best, was what I'd say was a six out of ten; she was kind of cute but completely unintimidating and, to be perfectly honest, a little forgettable. Luckily, she didn't see me with him and was none the wiser when I subtly crept up behind him to listen in on their conversation.

Initially, I'd been expecting Oliver to be his usual incredible self, but it seemed as if he'd suddenly had a personality transplant! I half-expected an imposter to reveal his true identity at any moment. Instead of that charismatic, funny guy I've described, Oliver was dull, boring, nervous and very forgettable. Consequently, as to be expected, the woman finally excused herself to go to the restrooms. At this point I actually felt sorry for her, as I know what it's like to have your Saturday night made a drag by a dull man who can't take the hint that he's boring you!

"What are you doing?" I asked Oliver when the woman had left.

"What do you mean?" he asked.

"Oliver, you are one of the funniest men I know," I told him, "and you're probably more intelligent than all the men in this room put together! So why are you coming across so dull?" Of course, I had no intention of hurting my friend, but he'd asked me to identify the problem – and I had!

"Look," he said to me. "She's gone to the restroom. Follow her in there and pretend you like me, make up something, like you saw me talking to her and you wanted to know if I was available. Try to find out what she says about me!"

It was a good idea, so I shot off to the restroom and there she was, looking in the mirror as she fixed her hair. "Excuse me." I smiled politely.

She smiled back.

"I know this sounds a bit strange, but I saw you talking to that guy at the bar, and I think he's pretty cute, so I was wondering if you two were an item. I mean, I don't want to step on anyone's toes, that's all," I lied convincingly.

She looked at me slightly bewildered for a second. "What guy?" She'd obviously forgotten all about the encounter that had taken place only moments ago!

"The guy you were just talking to, with the red shirt?"

She looked at the floor for a moment, and bit her lip as she tried to recall who I was talking about. Then she remembered. "Oh, him? No, I'm not with him. You're welcome to him."

"Oh, why? Is he a creep?" I asked, hoping that she'd say no as I didn't want to tell Oliver that.

"Oh no, nothing like that. He's a nice guy."

And there we had it. Like I said: nice guy = bland, forgettable, replaceable. She couldn't even remember him at all to begin with.

When I told Oliver what she'd said he took some time to think *about it. After a few days he told me he realised why he was presenting himself as the nice, boring, forgettable guy, even though he wasn't really like that. I was all ears.*

"It's like my friends who get drunk when they go and talk to women," he began. "They drink to the extent that they become something they're not."

"And what's that got to do with you?" I asked.

"Well, they get drunk to become someone so removed from who they actually are that, if and when they do get rejected, they can always say, 'Well, she only rejected me because I was drunk, she didn't get to see the real *me.' They prefer to have that excuse."*

It all clicked. I realised then that he was hiding behind this nice-guy mask so that he could console himself if a woman rejected him by saying, "Well, she didn't really reject me, *she rejected this nice-guy persona I put on."*

"That's a complete cop-out!" I said to Oliver.

"I know," he replied.

So remember – the nice guy is *not* the good guy, and being nice will only make you:

- **BLAND**
- **FORGETTABLE**
- **REPLACEABLE**

Be yourself is a terrible cliché that I hate. But in this case: BE YOURSELF AND STOP HIDING BEHIND THE MR NICE GUY PERSONA!

NEVER GOING BACK TO ZERO

The successful seducer understands that complacency and comfort lead to laziness.

MOST OF MY students share the same ultimate goal, which is to fall in love with a wonderful woman who, in turn, will love them forever – although most agree that, whilst searching for this woman, they want a lot of fun along the way! But there always comes a time when they find that one special woman who they'll want to spend the rest of their lives with and, when they do, the force of emotions they experience hits them like a car at 100 miles an hour! (Perhaps you've already experienced this?) Before long, the man will let the woman move in with him or vice versa and, before he knows it, they will be in a long-term relationship together. As a result, 'me' becomes 'us' and every decision made involves the two of them sitting down together to discuss things. The longer that relationship goes on, the more likely it will be that getting married and having kids is the inevitable outcome.

If this happens to you, then I want you make sure that *under no circumstances* will you ever let yourself go back to zero!

Some of my students come to me after a long-term relationship and say that they really thought they were going to be together forever. Most of them tell me that, when they came out of the relationship, they felt understandably very depressed but some told me the opposite – that they were, in fact, happy and excited to be back out in the field and hunting again.

However, the one thing they all agreed upon was that only by actually being out of the relationship could they see, for the first time in years, the extent to which they'd neglected nearly all other areas of their lives – their social lives, looks, interests, even their careers in some cases. They'd left the bubble that they were in and, as soon as they did, the reality of the situation punched them right in the head.

When men come out of a long-term relationship and experience this cold reality, they often feel that it's near impossible to get back into the 'dating scene' and to start attracting women again. The friends they used to hang out with would by now have moved on, either settling down in their own little relationship bubble or perhaps moving into new social circles. Remember: it's very common for men to neglect their friends and social lives when they get into a full long-term relationship and their friends subsequently feel almost abandoned. For example, they might ring up their newly loved-up friend and ask him to come out and hang with the guys, but he'll probably make excuses so that he can stay in with his girlfriend/fiancée/wife. As a result, his friends slowly give up asking and ultimately move on.

And now that he needs them again, he finds that it might be too late.

My students who have come out of long-term relationships often tell me that they no longer know what their hobbies and interests are. "We did everything together," is the common response. "We decided on things together, from holidays to pastimes to films, and I never really had time or space to do my own thing." Again, this is yet another area which men often neglect when in a fulltime relationship.

One of my students needed me to spend the first few lessons

just simply helping him work out what his opinions, likes and dislikes were. (He'd been married to a woman for 15 years who actually bullied him, which made his an extreme case.)

The other, more obvious area of neglect is physical appearance, and this is something women fall victim to even more than men do.

When we are with someone who loves us for who we are, it's a given that they will continue to love us even if our appearance takes a turn for the worse. As a result, we often stop taking care of our appearance, the weight slowly piles on – especially when we start having those cosy takeaways together in front of the TV. But, unfortunately, if the relationship ends, men go back to the real world, not only without much of a social life left but also not looking as hot as they did the last time they were on the dating scene – and this is why I teach my students who have not yet experienced a full-blown, long-term relationship that they must never neglect the other areas of their lives, never get complacent and never go back to zero.

The students who have experienced the break-up of a long-term relationship already know and understand this, and realise how much harder it will now be for them to move from zero and back up the ladder again. One of them, James, who was 35 at the time, had just broken up with the woman he was due to marry after a five-year relationship. When they split up, he informed me that he was initially very excited to return to the wild party animal he used to be and couldn't wait to meet new women. Unfortunately, however, things didn't go quite as well as planned.

JAMES: *When I finally left my fiancée, I felt as if a great weight had been lifted from my shoulders. We both had gotten too comfortable with each other, and the spark had left the relationship long ago. We both agreed to end it whilst we were still in our 30s, otherwise it would have been too late.*

The first thing I did was ring up my old mates who I hadn't seen for ages. I felt a bit guilty that I hadn't spoken to them for a while, but assumed they would understand the situation. Boy, was I wrong! Two of them had changed their numbers without telling me, and when I did eventually track them down they were full of excuses not to see me. One of them, at the end of our conversation, told me that I was getting payback for abandoning my mates for a woman. This jogged my memory, and I thought about all the times when my friends asked me to come and join them down the pub for some male bonding and I would always pass on the invitation – usually because my girlfriend wanted me to stay in with her. I always did as she said at the beginning because I didn't want to lose her.

My other friends had all settled down in a relationship also, some even had kids on the way, and so the last thing they wanted to do was go to nightclubs with me and chat up women. I found myself going on dating websites, which was okay to begin with, but the women seemed not to be interested in me when we actually met; they told me that they preferred men with more interests and hobbies, and that's when it dawned on me that I had stopped all of my old hobbies. I used to like car racing but I gave it up because my fiancée thought it was dangerous and had given me an ultimatum – either I quit car racing or she would leave. Again, I agreed to her wishes for fear of losing her. My other hobbies had also taken a backseat. This was because of the dull repetition I had gotten into in everyday life, which was coming home from work and then staying in with my fiancée in front of the telly. Anything we did outside of the home would be repetitive also; it would either be seeing other couples who were in the same position as us or going shopping for home furniture.

Our circle of friends was exactly like us! There was no variety at all!

Another wake-up call I received was when one of the women who I had met from the dating site told me that I looked nothing like the photo I had put up on my profile page. I realised that the photo I had up on there was taken four years ago and, since then, I had really let those takeaway meals catch up with me. It was horrible. I'd really let all the other areas in my life crumble, and it was all because I had gotten into a comfort zone that I had no intention of ever leaving.

I'm not boasting, but I used to be known as a bit of a ladies' man and women used to love how I was so witty and interesting. Now, women were telling me I was boring! I was no longer witty because I'd had no practice for so long. When you are with someone for a long time and are only hanging around with a small social circle, you start getting mentally lazy; you don't need to be witty or funny anymore – or even interesting. Before I got myself into this rut, I would meet new and interesting people all the time who would challenge me intellectually and, in doing so, keep forcing me to improve myself.

I gave up too much but, to be fair to my fiancée, she gave up a fair amount of herself for me too. At times, I wanted to go back to her out of fear that I would never meet anyone else, but I know being in a relationship for that reason is a big mistake.

Right now I'm dating a woman and it's still in the early stages, but I'm much more aware now than I used to be of remaining true to who I am. I've made new friends and, if she says she wants me to see her instead of my friends, sometimes I will say yes but that will only be because I genuinely want to see her that night and not my friends, not because I'm scared she will leave me. Even if one day I get married and have children, which is ultimately what I still want, I will make sure that I never leave myself vulnerable again and, most importantly, I will never stop being me.

I will never go back to zero again.

It took time for James to get back to being the man his fiancée fell in love with, the man that other women used to be so attracted to. It took time for him to make new friends and create a strong social circle. It took time for him to get back into physical shape. It took time for him to re-establish his interests and hobbies. It took time for him to get used to talking to complete strangers. But it didn't take him any time at all to realise that it was unacceptable to neglect all the other areas of his life for the sake of keeping a relationship – and it didn't take time to realise that getting into any kind of comfort zone can lead to complacency, laziness and, most importantly, the risk that he might have to start again from zero.

Compromising in some areas should not mean neglecting others.

WHAT IF SHE THREATENS TO LEAVE?

If a girlfriend threatens to leave you or go back to her ex-boyfriend, while you might want to cry or beg and ask her, "Why? What have I done? Can we fix this?" and other such needy statements, remember that she does not want to be the one coming up with all the answers. A little direction from your side will work better. The best thing that you can do is let her finish her list of reasons why she wants to leave (you shouldn't have to ask her, she will want to tell you). When she's finished, put your arm around her and say in your most sincere tone of voice that if she wants to leave then you will not stop her. Most importantly, you should follow it with something like this:

"Look, there's something I've always known, which is that, no matter what happens in my life, in the end I'll be happy. It's hard to explain, but the ultimate outcome for me will be happiness. Now if that means being happy with you, then great – if not, then so be it."

Give her a kiss, and even help her pack her stuff (if she is living with you).

This is the last thing I know you want to do, but it really is the most effective. Be strong when you do this; even if she complies, do not back down and start asking her questions or playing the pity card by crying or sulking. Very often, a woman will say she wants to leave simply to get a reaction out of you, and it's often a tactic she employs in order to make you appreciate her more. Although getting upset might serve the purpose of getting her to stay for a bit longer, men forget that it ultimately serves to elevate her position in the relationship significantly. From that moment on, you will have revealed to her that you *need* her, that you are willing to throw away your pride in order to keep her. She will remember this and use the 'I'm leaving you' line again and again, as I know from my own experience. However, whenever I've told a guy that I wanted to stop the relationship (usually to make him give me more attention), whenever his reaction was one of indifference, or even encouragement, I was always left contemplating whether or not I'd made a rash decision. Their reactions revealed that they were independent and strong enough to be happy with or without me. This, of course, increased the attractiveness of the men dramatically.

Bear in mind that she'll never expect this reaction from you, and will have prepared for all the reactions she presumed you were going to respond with. But not this!

As I've said before, the main quality women are looking for in a man is strength. And this can be a great opportunity to display that strength to the maximum.

However, the exception to the rule applies if you've done something really bad, like cheating on her. In these cases the rule still applies that you MUST NOT beg her to forgive you or cry. You can still display strength and non-neediness even in these scenarios.

Tell her that you know what you've done is bad, and that you wish you could turn back the clock and rectify the damage. Tell her that you care for her, which is why her pain upsets you so greatly. Make sure that she understands it was never your intention to hurt her, and that it never will be. Expect her to call you a number of names, as these are just reflections of her pain. Do not start believing that you're worthless, just because she's telling you that. Understand that it's only her pain (which you have caused) making her say these things.

When she has eventually calmed down – whether a week, a month or half an hour later – the best thing to say is this:

"Look, we have two choices here [make sure you say 'we' and not 'you']: either we allow this to ruin a great relationship, which in my honest opinion has the potential to grow to something even greater; or we make the decision to be stronger than this problem, and make a promise right now to one another that nothing will ever come between us again. From that moment on we only look to the future. I know what I want."

This is a powerful statement, as its terminology and structure will anchor her emotions in a positive way.

AUTHOR'S POSTSCRIPT

WHETHER YOU SIMPLY want to attract higher quality women or whether you're a complete beginner and have never even kissed a woman, I hope you'll find at least part of the solution to your problem within this book. My students range from the '40-year-old virgin' to the man who's already getting very hot women but still wants even more! I've taken into consideration that the men who read my book will, like my students, encompass a range of different levels of experience with women. And so I hope the information will be beneficial to you all, whatever your level of success so far.

I would like to thank all my friends, my ex-boyfriends, the naturals (whose brains I picked), fellow coaches and, of course, my students. Their points of view and insights have played an important role in providing the information contained herein.

I also want to thank the women who sat down and read my book before it was available for purchase. I enjoyed watching your faces drop in dismay at some of the things that I wrote, but enjoyed the moment more when you revealed to me afterwards that what I'd written was 'spot on!' It was interesting that a few of you asked me not to publish this, as you felt it gave away far too many of our secrets. That's when I knew that the content was really going to help the men out there.

This is literally the book that women do not want men to read!

I hope you've enjoyed it and, most importantly, that it's helped you and will continue to help you for years to come.

Enjoy your experiences!